SUSAN'S STORY

Susan's Story

An autobiographical account of my
struggle with dyslexia

❧❦❧

SUSAN HAMPSHIRE

St. Martin's Press
New York

First published in Great Britain by Sidgwick & Jackson Ltd.

Library of Congress Catalog Card Number: 82-60583

ISBN: 0-312-77966-6

First U.S. Edition
10 9 8 7 6 5 4 3 2 1

For
My mother,
my sisters Jane and Ann,
my brother John, and
my husband Eddie

ACKNOWLEDGMENTS

I should like to thank the following for their invaluable assistance: Joy Adams, my stand-in, for reading so many manuscripts; Donald Pavey, my cousin and lecturer in art and design, for information on learning techniques; Wendy Fisher and Vicky Vickers for information and help from the Dyslexia Institute; Jean Ross Mackenzie, my secretary, for typing the manuscript and correcting my spelling; Susan Schulman for sending across the Atlantic so many books and articles on dyslexia; and John Goldsmith for correcting my grammar.

SUSAN'S STORY

1

THERE IS a cocoon-like room that juts out from one corner of the house, an oblong brick extension with a large window looking on to the garden. This is my study. The walls are dark brown, with bookshelves on one side and pictures, packed tightly together like a patchwork quilt, on the other. From where I sit at my desk I can look up at the pictures and prints on the wall; and one on which my eye often rests is a framed clipping from *The Sunday Times* dated July 1971:

> It is the fate of a large number of dyslexics to be treated as morons, or mentally retarded, although they have normal distribution of intelligence and some well above average. Hans Andersen is known to have been dyslexic. Leonardo da Vinci and Einstein are said to have been, Edison probably was, and nearer home, one of our most successful young actresses, Susan Hampshire . . .

I don't claim that I look at this clipping every day but I am always aware that it's there. And on a 'bad day' it is a comfort to be reminded that August Rodin, Gustave Flaubert, W. B. Yeats, Woodrow Wilson and Nelson Rockefeller were also dyslexic.

A 'bad day' for me is a day when I have spent hours carefully embroidering 'Passionetly lovd' instead of 'passionately loved' on a corner of my husband's handkerchief.

Or a day when I have taken two right turns instead of two left turns on my way to Bermans, the theatrical costumiers, and become helplessly lost in the maze beyond Camden Town, finally arriving three-quarters of an hour late. Or when I find I have agreed to do a sixteen-week instead of six-week tour, having read six for sixteen in the contract. Or when I have forgotten how to spell 'phenomenon', 'psychology', 'pharmacy', and 'disciple', and can't think of any way of looking them up in the dictionary. Or when I have made five attempts at writing a simple thank-you letter and have ended up with:

Thank you it was a ~~delieghtfull~~ ~~deleightfull~~ ~~deleight-~~ ⌊ ~~ful~~ – it was lovely!⌋

Love,

S.

If you have read what I have written so far without any difficulty, your eyes gliding easily along the lines, seeing sentences as a whole, not flicking back, checking and re-checking the last few words; if you have not misread words, or read them in the wrong order, then it would happily appear that you and I do not have the same problem. My problem, and that of an estimated eleven per cent of people in Britain, is a specific reading and spelling difficulty. We are the people who see 'b' for 'd', 'f' for 't', 'because' as 'become' or 'before', 'no' as 'on', and so forth. When this problem was first investigated by two English doctors in 1876 it was called 'congenital word blindness'. Today it is called dyslexia, from the Greek *dys,* meaning ill, and *lexis,* meaning word. The fact that you won't find dyslexia defined in any dictionary is not just because the word has been so recently coined, but also because certain doctors are still arguing about whether it even exists.

The fact that I am a dyslexic has become fairly widely known, and people often ask me about it. One of the first questions they ask is: is dyslexia a disease? The answer is no, not in the sense that you can 'catch' it. It is a condition you have from birth.

Another frequent question is: does it exist in other countries, where they speak different languages and have different systems of writing – China and Japan, for instance? The answer is, yes, it does. Although Chinese and Japanese symbols are different from ours, although they write from right to left, and the pictorial basis of their writing is much easier for a dyslexic to understand, there is evidence that there are Japanese and Chinese dyslexics, but from the available figures it appears that they exist to a lesser degree than in the West.

A third frequent question is: is dyslexia hereditary? Yes, it is, usually handed down through the mother.

Yet another frequent question is: are dyslexics backward or unintelligent? No. They are often of above average intelligence; their problem is that the section of the brain governing language does not function properly.

After the average child has learnt to crawl and then to walk he will, with as much ease, at the age of five or so, learn to read and spell. A dyslexic child will also learn to crawl and walk, perhaps a little clumsily, perhaps using the left leg instead of the right for kicking a ball, but with as little difficulty as a 'non-dyslexic' child. Then the time comes for the dyslexic child to go to school. For no apparent reason he writes his b's and d's the wrong way round, or perhaps upside down, and he has enormous difficulty in learning to read and spell. His teachers are puzzled; he appears to be so bright and normal in every other way. Why does he not show the same enthusiasm for books as the other children? At home the non-dyslexic child will want to show off to his parents how he can read, but the dyslexic will say, 'You read – I love to hear you read', and many parents see nothing abnormal in this. After all, their little one is only six or seven, or eight, and surely there is nothing wrong in his wanting to be read to? Then suddenly he is nine, ten and eleven, and getting bad marks at school. His work is returned with incorrect spelling slashed through, and 'This work is not good enough', 'Lazy work', 'Do it again', written in red at the bottom. The child is becoming subdued and unresponsive, or the opposite – having tantrums.

If you are an enterprising parent you probably go to the library and you may have the good fortune to come across Professor T. R. Miles's book, *The Dyslexic Child*. This book will explain a great deal of what has puzzled you – but where do you go from there? Will the headmistress or headmaster think you are criticizing the teaching of the school, that you are an interfering, fussy parent? Where do you go for help? What does the future hold for your child? Does the educational system, as it stands, cater for your son or daughter? Maybe your child really is backward and lazy? Are you just a middle-class parent looking for an excuse?

Your child, if he is dyslexic, is neither backward nor lazy, and if his problem is spotted early enough – between five and ten – he can, with the right remedial teaching, be helped back into the conventional educational system. But if you have not spotted your child's needs, not tried to seek help, you may be in for a rough time, with distressing problems to deal with in the home, such as lying, temper tantrums, and truancy. Your child will be suffering so much at school from the other children's teasing and the teachers' disapproval that, of course, this will manifest itself in such behavioural problems. But, worst of all, the child will at the same time be losing confidence and begin to believe that he really is stupid, lazy, and backward, and that the people who are mocking him are right.

Though great strides have been made in the study and treatment of dyslexia in recent years, there is still a long way to go, and there are still far too many children whose lives are a misery. When I was a child, although the word dyslexia existed, research was not so advanced, teachers were not so enlightened, and help was far away. Yet I survived. I survived through the insight and the devotion of my mother, through the patience and love of my two sisters and my brother, and through my father's unusual attitude to life. It is almost entirely due to them not only that I have a story to tell, but that I am capable, however feebly, of telling it.

Last Summer I told my brother John that I'd been asked to write a book on dyslexia.

'Oh, that's nice,' he said, tongue in cheek. 'Who's going to write it? You can't.'

'What do you mean, I can't? I am!'

'You can't write.'

'But they're offering me an advance.'

'Well, take it,' he said. 'It's all you'll get. It'll never sell!'

* * *

To dot every 'i' and to cross every 't' in my career would only produce a 'Who's Who' of the theatre. But the story that I shall tell will show how so much of my working life has been greatly hampered by my disability. If this gives renewed hope to others with the same handicap, then the tale is doubly worth telling.

2

MUCH OF of my early childhood was spent under a baby Bechstein piano. I would curl up under the piano and listen to the dum, dum-der-rum, dum-der-rum overhead, the notes swelling as the loud pedal was squeezed down by a large foot in a cracked leather shoe, a few inches from my ear. Hearing this soothing thud, and watching my mother – slight, red-haired and energetic – giving private dancing lessons, I felt I was at the hub of things. To be part of my mother's working life, rather than to be left at home with a nanny, or an aunt, or a granny was, for me, perfection. My mother never resented me; I did not come between her and her work. I was content to sit quietly for hours listening to her, 'And plié two three, rise two three, on to the balls of the feet two three, stretch two three. Pull up those thighs. And again!'

She would often say, as she sat me on her knee, wrapping her arms tightly round me, 'You're such an easy child, so good – it makes life so easy.' Then she would put me back under the piano in the same way that most mothers tuck their child into a cot. I remember that I used to think how nice it was to be me, because my mother thought I was 'easy' – to be 'easy' in my mother's eyes was all important. I loved being under the piano, loved my mother, loved life. I must have been one of the most cuddled babies. As the youngest by far of four, I was always being heaved from

16

knee to knee, squeezed, kissed, and dandled. It was lovely. I was never alone.

At the end of the last class of the evening, my mother would brew herself a cup of tea.

'I must have a cup of tea,' she'd say. 'My throat . . . after all that teaching.' Then she would bundle me up in a car-rug and take me and my sisters home. But not always. If we were very quiet, and the caretaker didn't know, we would sleep in the studio, although, strictly, this was illegal, as 2 Basil Street, Knightsbridge, was supposed to be business premises.

The studio was large – forty feet square – white and high-ceilinged. It had a maple sprung-wood floor, specially laid on the advice of Anton Dolin, a friend of my mother's who often used the studio for practising. The floor was perfect for dancing, with a slight give, no splinters, and a surface that was smooth but never slippery. There were huge bomb-proof, wire-mesh windows that looked out onto the neighbouring rooftops, where my brother and I used to play hide-and-seek, crawling back into the studio on all fours, filthy, like wayward puppies. All the walls were covered by vast mirrors, and there were long horizontal bars, fixed at waist height, for ballet practice. In one corner was the Bechstein piano, often with a jug of flowers or leaves on it and, beyond, a great grey-green curtain which concealed the clothes-hooks, old chairs, and table that constituted the changing room.

On the left, on the way out of the studio, stood the cupboard where my mother made the tea, and where my sisters huddled and chatted while she gave the lessons. It was a quaint space, the shape of a pencil case or coffin. Someone once said that being in it was like being in a tomb, but for us, being so close to our mother, loving the smell of her scent that pervaded everything, it was like being in a womb – a womb-cupboard. Even my mother found the embrace of its four plaster-board walls comforting and she used it both as a kitchen and as a changing room. It contained a

17

couple of wobbly stools and shelves crammed with old ballet shoes, sewing things, dried milk, packets of tea, cups and saucers, net-and-petal hats, tights, red practice skirts, old leotards, and two electric rings. There was a permanent smell of dried glue – used for re-stiffening the points of ballet shoes after they had been darned for the umpteenth time – stew, tea, and sweat, which lingered in the nostrils even after one had gone down the stairs, out into the street, and onto a number 19 bus.

'Home' was a house in what was then the country, fifty minutes from London. It had a large garden and a dog that bit the postman. It was usually empty, since my brother and sisters were at boarding school, and by the time I was old enough to know the difference between a home and a cot, it was bombed.

My mother and father were both great workers. They believed in WORK. 'Better to wear out than rust out,' my mother would say, and it was amazing that she didn't wear out, for when I was a small baby and she was teaching in London she would get a train back to the country between classes. Our neighbour and I, in my pram, would be waiting for her at the station. She would sit down in the waiting-room, breast-feed me, then take the train back to London for her next class, while I was pushed, sleeping, back up the hill to the house.

At this time my father was working for I.C.I.'s General Chemicals Division in the North, and my mother was pursuing her career in London, so they seldom met. I didn't see enough of my father to feel that he was a strong part of those early days 'under the piano'. Had he been there, perhaps I would have had a more conventional start in life, like my sisters and brother, with a nursery, a nanny, walks in the park, birthday cakes and children's parties. Yet for me the tightly interwoven life of the studio was a wonder.

Eating, sleeping, playing, and watching my mother work, all in the same small area, was perfect. Even the meals, cooked in the cupboard on the two electric rings, perpetuated the magic of that mirrored room.

My mother would say daily, 'Eat up, Susan. This is full of goodness. Carrots are good for you – good for the eyes – eat up. And fish is good for the brain.' My mother was obsessed with the value of nourishment, and she was also obsessed with the brain, with having a good brain, using it and developing it. It is clear that the great attraction of my father had been his brain.

He was the son of a Yorkshireman, an Alderman of the City of Leeds, who owned a chain of greengrocery stores, the youngest of five – two boys and three girls. From an early age my father was hard-working and dedicated. He got a scholarship to Leeds Grammar School, and an exhibition to Oxford, where he got a first or perhaps it was a double first! Soon after he came down he joined Brunner Mond (later part of I.C.I.) and, by the time he retired, George Kenneth Hampshire had, without making much noise or fuss about it, worked his way up pretty well to the top of the company.

It was when he left Oxford that he met my mother, then a dancer with the D'Oyly Carte Opera. She too was the youngest in her family – she had six older brothers. Her father, Arthur Pavey, was a lawyer and her mother, born Jane Petley, had been a voluntary nurse in the First World War. They were fairly poor and lived in a small terraced house in Wimbledon. As my mother was a delicate child, and the only daughter, she was kept at home with her mother and had very little education. Apparently Granny would say to my mother, even when the sun was shining, 'There's a bit of a chill in the air, dear. With your health it's best to stay at home with Mother.' And so day after day of schooling was lost, and dancing lessons substituted.

I do not think either of my parents had had any previous attachments before they met, fell in love, and married. But soon after their marriage it was evident that two such dynamic personalities could not remain under the same roof.

My mother was determined not to end up like her own mother, a subservient housewife, who never left the house, her husband, or her children, except to go to church. She wanted more than that, and she had the intelligence and the personality to get it. Everyone was drawn towards my mother; she had a mysterious magnetism. People were bewitched by her, including, at the beginning, my father. He was quiet, withdrawn, thoughtful, and conventionally good-looking, blond and blue-eyed; my mother was small – 5 ft 2 ins – lively, fascinating and, though never beautiful, strangely sexy. Each should have been the perfect foil for the other. But no, their union was a positive clash!

My father's life was his work, and *vice versa*. Babies 'came along', as my mother would say, with great speed and by the time my brother, the third child, was born, my parents' work had begun to keep them apart, my father pursuing his career in I.C.I., in the North of England, my mother starting up her dancing school in London. They had been apart for some four years when I was conceived.

I have always marvelled at the story of my conception. I was a most unlikely 'afterthought', conceived mid-Atlantic as a result of my parents' attempt at a reconciliation. As a child I found it a strangely wonderful tale – I would sit at my mother's feet and beg her to tell me the story again and again.

'And then what happened? Were you pleased when I was born? Did Daddy come back? Why did they think I was a boy? What did Jane and Ann say? Tell me more. More about me!'

This was the story my mother told me.

One summer my father was going on business to America. My mother decided to save up her money, book a berth on the same ship, probably the *Mauretania* – and surprise him! When the ship was at sea, my father returned to his cabin to find my mother, wrapped in a belted camel-hair coat, sitting on his bunk. He had no option but to invite her to abandon the berth in steerage class that she was sharing with a woman and her child, and join him in his first-class cabin. On their arrival in New York he put her on the next boat home and they lived separate lives as before. Nine months later I was born. My father came to the nursing home to see me, where he was greeted with the news that he had a fine boy. This information was quickly proved to be inaccurate as soon as my parents took a closer look at me. The error had arisen owing to the fact that I had a pair of shoulders like a boxer!

My mother still loved my father, but a life together was impossible. These two remarkable individuals, both born achievers, simply could not find a roof broad enough to encompass them. My mother was an emancipated woman, born long before her time. She had so much to offer the world that I'm glad she did not succumb to domestic servitude. My father, for his part, could not allow his career to be hampered by family ties, and so they loved and parted, but never divorced.

This had very little effect on me as I never knew them as a couple, but my two sisters, and especially my brother, did suffer from the break-up and missed their father terribly. They had known family life: Daddy gardening at the week-ends, with the children pushing the wheelbarrow; roast beef and Yorkshire pudding for lunch on Sunday; rushing to the door, with the dog, to greet him when he got home from work. When I arrived in the world my sister Jane was already the head of the family and my brother John, the only man. It all seemed fine to me. I didn't know that four hearts in the South had pieces missing, and another heart in the North was pining. But it had to be – Mr and Mrs Hampshire were not compatible.

Some people probably thought of us as a moderately well-off family in comparison to most, but we always felt poor. We were never short of food, but our clothes were all hand-me-downs and we never had anything that was not essential. The beautiful Bechstein piano was essential, but the remainder of our belongings were pleasantly 'make do', comfortably shabby. 'We can't afford it,' was a very familiar sentence, though it was not resented.

I have always felt that never to be rich, and above all never to feel rich, is a great advantage in life. The necessity to work in order to survive is essential to me and I have never regretted that there were so few luxuries and frills in our childhood. Even a chocolate biscuit was an enormous treat, and not simply because it was just after the war when rationing was still in force: my mother had given birth to four monstrously sweet-toothed brown-eyed children. She knew how to fill our hearts with wistful longing just by showing us her biscuit-filled tin box, usually hidden under the sheets and towels in the linen skip. The tin was a little rusty, as I remember, and was always kept 'until the children are home from boarding school'. I, of course, was at home – and twelve weeks with those chocolate biscuits suffocating under the sheets in the skip were agony for me.

Jane, the eldest, was an amazingly positive and patient sister, with the plaited auburn-gold hair of a girl in a medieval painting. She could wait for the opening of the rusty biscuit tin with more ease than the rest of us. With the same ease she found it impossible to fail an exam, impossible not to win first prize or be anywhere but top of her class. Without flurry or sentiment she put herself in charge of the Hampshire offspring and led us boldly.

Ann, the next sister down, petite like my mother, and with the same inner fire, had the sweetest tooth of all. Luckily she cooked so well that she could make sweets out of breadcrumbs. Music was her great love and, like the rest of the family, she found all academic work easy, especially maths. Her dark shining hair, always looking special, inspired everyone to say, 'Ann, such a dear little thing, so pretty'. She took me on, or rather she was the sister burdened with looking after me. She ironed my hair ribbons (until I was eight, when my mother said, 'Surely you're old enough to look after your own school ribbons', so I did, by wrapping them round the hot pipes in the bathroom), held my hand

22

when we were out, and gave me nick-names and money.

My brother John, who also had the family sparkly brown eyes, found school work easy too. He didn't seem to have to work very hard to learn the eight languages he speaks fluently, or remember all the dates in a history book. Considering that he had to live with three sisters and his mother, he survived very well. He kept me in my place – without a father around I could have, and probably did, become unbearable. Sweets were not the main focus of John's life, so he made an excellent guard of the tin box.

It was difficult for us all to live in the studio in the holidays, so my mother usually took us camping – even at Easter – in Scotland, where the winds were so strong that I carried canvas bags filled with rocks to prevent my being blown away. The magical tin went with us, and at night was carefully hidden away, in case of mice – or children.

The tin was checked every dawn by my brother and sisters. One morning, after the cows had woken us by putting their heads through the tent flaps, it was discovered that a mouse had managed to open the tin and eat its way through every biscuit. Imagine! Thirty biscuits of every variety, all eaten by one mouse. John looked up grimly and asked, 'Who's eaten Mummy's biscuits?'

A very small person, with a very nasty red face, stared into her milk and said:

'I 'spect the mouse ate them 'cos I didn't.'

My brother pounced on me at once. I was hardly big enough to hold my mug but I defended both myself and the lie.

'A mouse ate the biscuits, I heard it – I promise. I didn't eat the biscuits!'

My brother laid me flat on the ground and sat on me.

'I'll push your eyes out if you don't tell the truth.'

'The mouse ate them, I promise.'

Jane and Ann were coming to my rescue, pulling John off me, while my mother checked that the tin really was empty. It was. Now everyone was ready for war. It was the only time I can remember when my family was not prepared to indulge me beyond belief.

'Well,' my mother said, as she took the kettle off the fire, 'it was a very silly mouse, because all those biscuits were filled with . . .'.

'Yes,' I interjected, 'wasn't it a silly mouse . . .' and then my mother continued, '. . . those biscuits were filled with mouse poison. I wanted to catch that mouse. I've suspected her for some time!'

I let out a yell, and cried, 'Oh Mummy, Mummy, *mouse* poison . . . Will it kill me?' John threw me onto the ground-sheet again, but Jane and Ann scooped me up and frog-marched me behind the tent to help me to be sick. No more was ever said.

3

MY MOTHER's decision not to send me to school in the
ordinary way was, quite literally, my salvation. Since I had
not been to a kindergarten, or play group as we would call
it now, there was no indication whatsoever that I might
have difficulty in learning, yet by the time I was five my
mother had made up her mind that no school would be
suitable for me. It must have been very largely a gut
reaction on her part, the product of a strong and very
shrewd maternal instinct. Another factor may have been
that the atmosphere in London was tense: the war was
over, but it had left a country frayed and clinging to its
children. My mother was still on her own, the three older
children were at boarding schools – perhaps she was loath
to see her youngest slip from her grasp.

The studio in Knightsbridge had become virtually our
only home. We lived quite happily in sleeping-bags at night,
using what we called a 'billy-can' for a loo, as the proper
lavatory was outside the studio, three flights up the stairs.
At Christmas, the table, which was usually behind the
curtain across the alcove, was dragged to the middle of the
studio floor, and we sat round on assorted chairs amidst a
theatrical display of multi-coloured decorations, some of
which had belonged to my grandmother, but most of which
were improvised from crêpe paper, feathers and cut-up
newspapers.

But from now on the table was to be dragged out every morning so that four-, five- or six-year-olds could do their lessons at what was the birth of an extremely successful school.

My mother, despite her own limited education and her commitment to the dancing school, was driven by some inspired obsession. Once she had resolved to start a school, she telephoned a few friends and asked them if they would like her to start off their children's formal education.

As every inch of the studio walls was covered with mirrors, when we looked up from our school-books it seemed as if the room was filled with thirty children. Staring into the mirrors, watching what everyone in the room was doing without turning my head, and spying behind me was wonderful.

We were all given pencils, from a jar in the middle of the table, and a piece of paper. It was hard to write on the paper as it slipped on the wood grain of the table but, with our heads bent and our eyes only a few inches away from the sheet in front of us, we drew, or copied letters and numbers. But too often I found my eye wandering to the white china globes that covered the lights on the high ceiling, wondering when would it be time for milk and a biscuit. It was easy to talk about what I had seen in the park, or to sort out the ballet shoes, or to put books away neatly according to size, but to decipher the alphabet, or recognize C.A.T. and say what it spelt was almost impossible. I could concentrate on some tasks, like putting away the music in the piano stool or finding the pianist's cushion. When I was required to write, a strange feeling came over me, and I felt that there was a long piece of string in my head.

My mother would say, 'C.A.T. spells cat. Susan, what does C.A.T. spell?'

'I don't know. I don't know, Mrs Hampshire (as I called her at school), I don't know what it spells.'

The string inside my head stopped me from answering. It actually felt as though my skull housed a whole ball of string, with an end sticking out of my crown. I thought that if I pulled at this, I could get the string out, empty my head of it, unravel the tangle in my brain. I felt that I could pull it out inch by inch. Every day, I could feel the string coming out, and I would think to myself, 'Soon it'll be gone.'

I longed for the day when there would be no more string in my head – it was so heavy. I wondered if everyone had a ball of string, the other children, my mother. Did her silky red hair hide a ball of string? Yet I never noticed anyone else pulling at the middle of his head to get rid of his string. Was I the only one? And if so, was it a good or a bad thing to have string?

'Mummy, I can feel my string.'

'Don't be so ridiculous, Susan.'

The page, the pencil, my mother's face, her slightly oily skin – not a line on it – her dark brown eyes compelling me to answer correctly, her nail polish half erased by the washing-up, all this I could see and remember – but I could not remember C.A.T. Probably the most difficult word in the world, C.A.T. If only the other children couldn't spell C.A.T.

'Stop looking in the mirror and think about how you spell cat.'

I couldn't. I just could not. I tried, but I couldn't. My head was empty – except for the string.

By the end of the first year my mother had recruited about twenty more children for the winter term and had hired a church hall behind Harrods.

I did not relish the proposed change. No more mirrors. No more noisy dragging of the table across the studio floor and grabbing the chair opposite the best mirror to watch my mother, in her full skirt, stooped over the table helping someone with C.A.T. No more creeping out of a sleeping-bag in the morning, watching the breakfast cooking in the cupboard, and eating it off the Bechstein piano (the marks are on the wood to this day). No. There was to be a four-room flat in Dolphin Square, with a kitchen a little bigger than the cupboard, and two bathrooms. Goodbye 'billy-can'.

School was to be in the church hall at St Saviours, Knightsbridge, with two teachers – my eldest sister had just left school and was to help my mother out. There were hymns, and a register, and a noisy bell. Mrs Hampshire's School was taking shape and, for me, it was the wrong shape. I loved the squashed life of the studio.

In the new school we silently copied my mother's best writing on lined paper. It was not copper-plate or Italian script, but fine, curly writing in red crayon, and we made G's and A's all down the page. I enjoyed it now, it was rather like drawing. Soon we were putting three letters together to make a word. But somehow the letters we put together never made me think of the word. They didn't make me think of anything. AND, or CAT, or THAT, or IF, or SO, or THE, especially THE, could have been any group of letters – they could have been anything at all – a secret code. Perhaps one day in five my brain recognized the code, saw the secret for a moment, and I could put my hand up excitedly and say, 'I know how to spell cat! T.H.A.T.' And as I said it, I knew I was wrong, but my memory had gone.

'Now Susan. Again. How do you spell cat? It's not T.H.A.T. It's C.A.T. See a cat, pretend to stroke a cat, write cat. Now Susan, what does C.A.T. spell?'

I didn't know. C.A.T. meant nothing. The letters meant nothing, the sound meant nothing.

I don't remember if it disturbed me – perhaps it did. I often woke up with my whole body in a sweat, and found I'd wet my bed. Sleeplessness and bed-wetting are fairly common with dyslexic children, and my distress was mild in comparison to many other children. I did not have screaming fits, or tantrums. But then, thanks to my mother, I wasn't struggling to survive in a class of thirty; we had one teacher to every five pupils.

The other children seemed to find cat easy, they remembered cat from one day to the next. They were kind, they didn't laugh at me and if they did, they were told to stop. It was this protection, this cushioning, that made bearable my life between the ages of five and fifteen. In the real world, it would have been very different. I was encouraged in other activities, I was constantly told I shone at dancing.

I must have been eight or nine when my brother got me to tell his friends how I spelt my name.

'Listen to how my sister spells her name. How do you spell Susan Hampshire?'

Long pause.

'S.H.'

Peals of laughter.

I thought that meant that I'd done it well. I was proud of myself. S.H. Yes, that's how I spell my name. They're laughing because it's good.

This blinkered attitude saved me again and again. This, and the fact that my mother insisted on giving me dancing lessons every day of my life from the age of three onwards, thus helping to train my brain through movement, giving me good physical coordination, eliminating clumsiness and awkwardness, laying the foundations of hope.

As yet none of us really knew that there was a problem – but doubts were seeping in everywhere. At night I would lie awake and listen to my sisters and mother talking as they corrected the books, discussed a new time-table, or prepared lessons for the next day, and often I heard the words 'retarded' or 'mental'. Could these refer to me? What was 'retarded', what was 'mental'? Were they special? I'd wander in and say I couldn't sleep, in the hope of hearing more.

'Are you still awake, you naughty girl? Get back to bed at once.'

And I'd stomp back to bed and try to sleep. But . . . retarded . . . mental . . . what did it mean? Was it special?

In the morning I'd creep into each bed in turn for a cuddle and, perhaps, further information. Jane's bed was always beautifully warm. With her milky white skin she was Junoesque. She'd tolerate me for a bit, but then my constant fidgeting would annoy her and she'd turn me out and I'd go along to Ann's bed. There was almost nothing in Ann's room except her piano and a bed, but it was surprising that they both managed to fit in, it was so small. Ann always slept with the window wide open, the air blowing on to her face. Her bed was so cosy and the material of her nightdress so soft. She'd curl me up and I'd sleep like a kitten for a while. Then,

'Ann, what is retarded?'

'Shh . . . go to sleep.'

'But it's morning.'

No response. So I'd climb out and try my mother.

'Mummy, if I make you a cup of tea, can I get into bed for a cuddle?'

My mother slept in the sitting room, amongst all the books, on the sofa. It was a great squash to get in and very uncomfortable for her, and for me.

'Mummy, what's retarded?'

'Don't ever mention that word. People will think you are mental!'

She would put paid to any further discussion by getting out of bed and pretending to be busy – perhaps going over to her desk and sorting through the great pile of school bills, most of which she never sent out to the parents. (One result of my mother's inability to charge parents for the education their children were receiving was that the flat was full of portraits of the family. Many of her pupils were the sons and daughters of portrait painters, like Anthony Devas, Robin Guthrie, and Robert Buhler, and she found it easier to accept a canvas, in lieu of payment, than to send in her account.)

And so, for a time, the word 'retarded' remained a mystery.

In the holidays there was also my brother John's bed to crawl into when I was doing my round.

This was not so easy. To boys of twelve or fourteen, little sisters are a pest at the best of times, but at 6.30 in the morning they are the worst kind of vermin.

'John can I get into your bed for a bit?'

'Only if you shut up and don't fidget.'

I'd crawl in and clasp my arms round his waist and try not to move.

Then he'd cry, 'Get off, take your hands off. Don't touch me. Now go to sleep or get out.'

The argument would rise to a crescendo, and my mother would come in.

'Mummy, Susan's annoying me. Tell her to get out.'

What a nightmare it must have been for them, this creature padding from room to room in the morning wanting to get into their bed and wanting to know the meaning of the word retarded.

4

THE THEORY is that dyslexia is handed down through the female line, usually to sons; there are ten per cent more dyslexic boys than girls. But of course, none of this had been investigated when I was a child, so the question of whether my mother was herself dyslexic never arose. She started her school for me when I was about five, and for ten years I remained in her, and my sisters', good care. Every morning of those ten years my mother called out the school register, and every morning she read out almost every name incorrectly.

We stood in St Saviours Church Hall, about sixty of us by the mid-1950s, in crinkly bottle-green wool uniforms, to say 'Our Father', and then to sing, 'Thank you for the world so sweet'. I was often asked to sing solo one of the verses. My voice was clear and tuneful, and my mother accompanied me on the piano, playing a great many wrong notes as she refused to cut her nails. Sometimes my sister Ann would accompany me, playing beautifully and smiling encouragingly at me. After school she would give me extra practice on the *Messiah* by the piano in her bedroom as she said that I had perfect pitch and a good voice. This could have been to give me confidence in other subjects – whatever the reason, I enjoyed singing more and more.

When hymns were over, Mrs Hampshire would read the register. Mrs Hampshire wore a mink coat, bought just

after the war in a Harrods sale, on a staff discount – she had
worked at Harrods for some weeks during the sale in order
to get it. She almost never took the coat off and it smelt
lovely, of old scent, and her. She always wore it for the
register, which went something like this:

Lydia Baathurst	– (Linda Bathurst)
Batric Peckwith	– (Patricia Beckwith)
Tane Bayfurs	– (Jane Beyfus)
Martin Buhler	– (Michael Buhler)
Tom Dell	– (Tom La Dell)
Esro Devas	– (Esmond Devas)
Anthony Towel	– (Anthony Dowell)
Carole Bowell	– (Carole Dowell)
Anthony Elot	– (Anthony Elliott)
Rose Elot	– (Rosemary Elliott)
Mania Gingud	– (Maina Gielgud)
Linny Guthy	– (Lynette Guthrie)
Alex Gutty	– (Alexander Guthrie)
Shusan Ampshire	– (Susan Hampshire)
Simone Tangle	– (Simone Nangle)
Patrick Tangle	– (Patrick Nangle)
Susam Stranks	– (Susan Stranks)
Sarah Wolp	– (Sarah Wolpe)

These pronunciations varied from day to day and
throughout the year. If we heard a name that was even
vaguely like our own, we would say 'here'. No one giggled,
or even seemed surprised. But, looking back, I have to
conclude that my mother was more than slightly dyslexic,
though not severely – she was always taking correspondence
courses and, at about forty-five, started work for a degree
in Latin. To my mother Latin and Greek were synonymous
with good education and wisdom. Was this or that word
derived from the Greek or Latin? It was most important to
my mother that I should know these things.

'No one will ever think you're retarded or a fool if you
do. It's indifference in life that . . .'

'But Mummy!'

She'd cut me short. I was not allowed to protest when she'd set her mind to something.

'Go and look it up in the dictionary. Look up "indifferent".'

I dreaded being asked to look something up, even a number in the address book. I would slide off with one of the eight Oxford Dictionaries that littered our little box of a sitting-room, along with mountains of uncorrected exercise books, unposted bills and unfinished cups of tea, and go into the bathroom. I would sit on the lavatory seat (still my favourite place to work) and gaze at the dark blue book. After twenty minutes of to-ing and fro-ing amongst the soft, slithering pages, I would have to go back to my mother and admit, 'I can't find "indifferent".'

'Try!'

So back I went to the bathroom. Was it 'endefarint', 'endifarent', or 'endeferent'? It could be absolutely anything. Eventually I'd slope back to the sitting room.

'What comes after E.N.D.?'

'*Ind*ifferent – think, think, say the word *ind*ifferent. How does it sound? What's that first letter? What's the sound of the first letter? It's "I", isn't it? Go back and look up I.N.D.'

And so it dragged on, an hour, an hour and a half, two hours, shuffling between the sitting-room and the bathroom, sitting on the plastic lid, now warm, looking out of the window at the river, clutching the book, and saying to myself, 'I can't look up "indifferent", I don't know how to spell "indifferent", I can't even find the I's.'

There are no set patterns for people with spelling difficulties. They will spell 'indifferent' three ways in the course of one paragraph, know it one day and not the next.

In 1975, while acting as presenter for a B.B.C. documentary on dyslexia, I met Professor Miles, the author of *The Dyslexic Child*. To illustrate the sort of spelling errors a dyslexic child produces I quote an example given in Professor Miles's book, together with his comments:

There are many strange and fasen (t crossed out) ating fisf, but it seems difecolt to belever that some fish are kapabul of generating ther (crossings out) whone ELEstricaty wh (crossed out) with which they can guve (?) a shoc .... these fish have an orgen behind eash (changed to each) ire which is a mase of sels, roth like a hone kome.

(There are many strange and fascinating fish, but it seems difficult to believe that some fish are capable of generating their own electricity with which they can give a shock .... These fish have an organ behind each ear which is a mass of cells, rather like a honeycomb.)

There whars on anser to this ecsept the noding of a fyuw heads and the ciking of the smallest sistes a ganst the tadule. And of curs it wars truw, the chulgren war thin and poor and they never had enuf to eat. The onie father had bide in a storm a foue years Be for.

(There was no answer to this except the nodding of a few heads and the kicking of the smallest sister's [foot] against the table. And of course it was true. The children were thin and poor and they never had enough to eat. Their own father had died in a storm a few years before.)

A dyslexic child will often spell a word in several different ways on successive occasions: Henry's inconsistencies over 'fish' are examples. Also syllables may be omitted or put in the wrong order, as in 'elestricaty' for 'electricity'. Sometimes losing the place takes the form of repeating a word or syllable, as in the repetition of the word 'a' in the first passage; and sometimes there seems to be no clear sense of where one word ends and another one begins, as in 'a ganst' for 'against' and 'Be for' for 'before'. It is these kinds of errors, as well as the b–d confusion, which often give the spelling of dyslexic children its bizarre character.

It is, however, highly intelligent spelling. Given that one cannot remember how a word is spelled, one can still sometimes *deduce* the correct spelling by sounding the parts of the word to oneself, and this is in fact what Henry appears to have been doing. Even when the spelling is totally wrong, as in the 'fyuw' for 'few', it is often possible to see the logic behind it; and from the phonetic point of view many of his attempts, even when wrong, are remarkably accurate.*

I have often noticed that when dyslexics read, they do not take in what the words mean even if they have been able to read them out loud.

For instance, the sentence, 'The visitor to an art arena game is confronted with an enormous piece of paper covering one wall of the room,' may be read as , 'This visit too can art . . . *game is confined* (to an) enormous paper (. . . word missed out . . .) on one wall (. . . word missed out . . .).'

As for obvious reasons I did not shine at school, I had to find an alternative means of survival. Making friends with the cleverest children in the class was one way. When I was invited to tea by a friend I was so pleasant to the parents, so well behaved – helping to clear the table and wash up – that when the time came for homework, my friends would willingly allow me to copy from them. In exchange, with the half-a-crown I had 'borrowed' from my mother's purse (in the end she slept with her handbag under her pillow to stop the pilfering), I would buy them presents – little glass animals, all the rage then, or sweets.

This need to give, for fear of otherwise not being tolerated, has remained with me all my life. I desperately wanted to be liked and I assumed that no one could like someone as 'stupid' as me. To this day, as much of a third of my hard-

<hr>

* *The Dyslexic Child* by Professor T. R. Miles, published by the Priory Press in 1974.

earned income disappears in this way, in buying the right to friendship. Nothing has changed; the doubts of childhood remain. I don't pretend that if this need did not exist I would be rich, but I would at least have been able to save, and perhaps not have to work for the rest of my life. If it started with the desire to be 'liked', it developed through a feeling of guilt at the thought that, despite everything, I had been so lucky in adult life.

Another method of survival in childhood was to try to be different or amusing, and this is where my hamster, Whiskatina, came in. She was originally called Whiskers, but when I took her out of her cage a few weeks after I got her, I discovered four baby hamsters and, of course, she became Whiskatina. Whiskatina was a subtle distraction. Much of her life was spent in my cardigan pocket, when she wasn't producing. When it was my turn to stand up and read Shakespeare aloud, I would take her out of my pocket and put her on the table in front of me. She would conveniently be at her most endearing, stuffing her cheeks with the dried peas and grain I had thoughtfully provided, then carefully washing her whiskers with her pink paws. Every head would turn towards her. She was a placid creature and would continue her eating and washing, unaware of her audience, occasionally knocking the odd pea on to the floor.

Sometimes I felt that my teacher condoned this distraction, wanting to help me out of the painful business of reading Shakespeare, a cruel task for a poor reader. She would allow Whiskatina to take her time with the peas, waiting, with her arms folded and head on one side, for the return of order. By the time Whiskatina's performance was over, the bell would go and we would move on to the next class. As we got up to go my teacher would take me aside to say quietly, 'That was very silly, Susan. You can't always get out of reading. You know it is extremely cruel, not to say distracting, to keep a hamster in your pocket – how unnatural and unkind to that poor little creature. Please, in future, keep her in a proper cage at home.'

This I did, and I bred from her, bringing her babies to school every seven weeks to sell as an alternative form of distraction – one shilling for each baby, and the day strategically chosen to coincide with the lessons I found the most difficult.

Yet another means of gaining acceptance was my unending willingness to do the messy jobs, like sweeping the floor after lunch, clearing away the chairs, stacking the books and helping the younger children put on their coats. I always had a pencil, rubber, pencil-sharpener, or piece of blotting-paper at hand to lend to the teacher I wanted to please. My rules were: be easy, set a good example in the classes where you are not completely hopeless, like singing and games; at rounders always be a good sport and fight ferociously for your team; get the extra round even if you twist your ankle or fall over and get mud all over your dress; be a keen participant in everything and never object to having the worst job, like fielding, or supervising the little ones, or being a reserve; cheer the others on; think up terrific adventure games for break and give everyone in your gang a sweet (bought with stolen money) when they join. If you are inventive, loving, always smiling and laughing, people will forget that you are stupid and don't know what mental and retarded mean.

All this was done by instinct rather than by design, and sometimes my devices didn't work, sometimes I could not avoid my turn and had to stand up and read Shakespeare aloud. I hated Shakespeare from those days up to 1975, when I played my first Shakespearean part, Kate, in *The Taming of the Shrew,* opposite Nicky Henson. As a child I thought that Shakespeare was a man who wrote plays that were very difficult to understand and even more difficult to read. I excluded his work from my consciousness. I thought that the plots were silly, put together in a way that made guessing impossible, and that the language was too full of unpronounceable words. I hated Shakespeare because I was frightened of his words. It has taken me a long time to learn that the better a part is written, the easier it is to act. Shakespeare does so much of the actor's work for him by making the words so rich. Shakespeare is a joy to me now but, in my mother's classroom, it was a torture. When I did eventually stand up to read I could not see, understand or say more than one word in five. My friends laughed, my cheeks grew hot and sweat trickled down my arms into little patches on the floor. I closed the book, they stopped giggling, and I sat down. Quiet humiliation. I thought, 'One day they'll respect me. One day I'll be famous, and I'll go into Harrods with a shopping basket and have enough money to have an account, and a car will be waiting to drive me away. I'll be like Elizabeth Taylor. Everyone knows and admires her.'

My mother must often have witnessed scenes like this, and she was brilliant at doing a 'cover-up job' to protect me. But even her marvellous patience had its limits and often, in despair, towards break-time she would send me off to Harrods with a list of things needed for the school lunch. She hoped the practical experience of shopping would replace the academic work I should have been doing. But it taught me cunning, not arithmetic.

In my straw boater and green uniform I would set off through Harrods, happy to be free. If I saw anyone I knew, the mother of one of the children at school, for instance, I would pretend not to be me, try to make her think that I was a child from another school by appearing to be barmy. I would drag a hand into my blazer, twist my face into a grimace and limp through the departments until I was out of sight. Then I would continue with the shopping, chatting to the sales assistants, skipping and working out a way that I could wangle sixpence out of the change without actually stealing or telling a lie. In the end I always had to do both, but taking money never seemed like stealing – it was a necessary part of survival.

*   *   *

39

Visits to my father were fairly infrequent, perhaps once a year, usually at Christmas. I saw so little of my father that a trip to his flat in Liverpool was a great treat, marred by only one thing: his endless questions about algebra. My father thought that algebra was of paramount importance.

One Christmas John and I arrived in Liverpool at about lunch-time and were met at the station by my father, now Chairman of his division of I.C.I., and Hollins, his chauffeur.

'I expect you two children have eaten,' my father said, and before we'd had time to protest that we were starving, he continued, 'Good – thought you had. We'll shop – then I can free Hollins for the holiday.'

The Liverpool food market was a series of great Victorian arcades, lined with stalls, and the aisles were strewn with fruit and vegetables that had rolled out of their boxes or simply been thrown away. I remember on this occasion my father amazed us by taking us on the most wonderful spree. In his impeccably tailored suit ('Had this over thirty years, since I left Oxford – and these shoes'), he walked in front, John and I behind him, and Hollins, I think, with a string bag and brown paper carrier, brought up the rear.

'Two carrots on the ground on the right,' my father muttered. I was on the right flank, so I dodged down, picked up the stray carrots, and popped them into one of Hollins's bags.

'Potatoes on the left,' my father murmured.

John scooped up six unwanted potatoes from the stone floor and gave them to Hollins.

'Hollins, John, get those leeks and onions. Susan, we need more carrots.'

At the end of fifteen minutes the bags were full and we stopped for a pound and a half of bacon scraps and some sausage-meat, and two pounds of greens.

My father lived in the top half of a small rented semi-detached house on the outskirts of Liverpool. There was a sitting-room, a box-room and a bedroom, plus a kitchen and a bathroom – all minute. Every surface seemed to be painted brown, the flat was a mud-like haze from one end to the other, and the beds were always damp. The box-room was filled with wine, boxes of oranges and apples, Christmas gifts from I.C.I., and empty wooden crates that father was saving to put to good use.

Hollins wished us all a Happy Christmas, and presented my father with a small, wrapped present. In return Daddy stuffed some large white five pound notes into his hand and gave him a bottle of Scotch. Hollins waved, tipped his hat, slipped into the driving seat and drove to his own house, which was probably twice as large and grand as my father's. After Hollins had gone we unwrapped the turkey, put our spoils from the market on the kitchen table, got the apples and oranges, a gift from the firm, from the box-room and gazed with hungry anticipation at the ingredients of a perfect Christmas dinner.

Table decorations, candles, hats, crackers, streamers, sweets, chocolates and silver threepenny bits in the pudding – these were the finer touches we had only when we were with my mother. But we did have crystallized fruit and a plum pudding, donated by I.C.I. and my father's landlady respectively. When I tried to raise the subject of threepenny bits, he asked, 'Do you think I'm made of money?' We didn't dare say 'Yes.'

When given the order, John and I would light the fire and draw up the worn 'utility' armchairs. John lazed back in his chair, smiling and waiting, looking forward to my father's inevitable bombardment of questions about my progress at school. I sat on my father's lap, my arm limply folded round his neck, my heart springing out of my chest, dreading what was to come. Algebra. It meant so much to my father, and nothing to me. The ball of string was filling my head, from ear to ear. The questions started and I could not answer. My father looked at my blank face and I moaned, 'Daddy, I can feel a ball of string in my head.'

'Don't be stupid,' he said, 'Come on, Susan, *think*.'

As the interrogation crawled on, I resorted to pulling gently at a long hair in my father's right ear, 'accidentally' tugging at it. Anything to distract him!

'Susan, stop that. Concentrate. What is the square root of . . .'

Another tug – and he pushed me off his lap, his interest in my knowledge of algebra overtaken by fears for his personal safety. My poor father!

But my back was against the wall. My only hope was to divert his attention through cunning, quickness of mind, the ability to distract by the unexpected – a quick pirouette, a joke. I suggest a cup of tea and everyone gives up. My brother smiles and sinks deeper into his chair. My father slaps my bottom and pushes me off to the kitchen. John is delighted: not only have I failed, but I've also got to leave the warm to make the tea.

The kitchen was at the far end of a cold corridor and, as my father thought it was wasteful to use matches, we had to make a spill from an old newspaper, light it from the fire, then creep, hand cupped round the flame, along eighteen feet of draughty passage to the kitchen. There we would light the Heath Robinson gas stove and put the oldest black tin kettle in existence on to boil. I don't know what my father was earning at that time, but as a Divisional Chairman of I.C.I., he could presumably have afforded matches, and an up-to-date gas stove, and probably a whole house and two maids to run it. It wasn't that he was mean; meanness didn't enter into it. It was simply Yorkshire frugality.

'Daddy, can I have a match? The spill's gone out for the fifth time.'

'Money doesn't grow on trees you know. Your mother is very extravagant.'

(This was the most derogatory thing I ever heard him say about my mother, who was hardly extravagant on the money that he gave her for the four of us.)

'Then there are three of you children at boarding school – and the tax man takes 19/6d in the pound. Of course you can't have a match.'

Curiously, my father did leave only a modest amount when he died, which was shared amongst the family. The only real extravagance he was ever known to indulge in was a second-hand Rolls Royce, which he bought after he retired. When he was on the main board of I.C.I. and living permanently in London, instead of buying a house or flat he took over my first bachelor-girl service flat in Langham Street, and on Sundays he would cook roast beef for lunch for John and me – he was a wonderful cook. Afterwards we would listen to the radio and laugh a lot. When it was time to go he'd clasp my hand and say, with tears in his eyes:

'I hope you're still a virgin.'

5

CHILDREN EXPERIENCING learning difficulties often live with an additional threat looming over them: the prospect that the holidays too will be a nightmare, a nightmare created by over-anxious parents insisting on holiday lessons to improve their child's academic performance. But here again I was lucky. As a child I had many amazing, joyful, interesting and (of course) inexpensive holidays. I do not remember one where I felt I was expected to 'catch up'. I suppose my mother knew it was hopeless! Instead, she devised the sort of holidays that would replace, through practical experience, the knowledge that was escaping me at school.

She dreamed up a wonderful variety of 'adventures' – camping, walking, living on a farm, travelling abroad on tuppence ha'penny, and later earn-your-keep holidays, like helping in stables and cooking. We never had the standard English holiday in the standard English hotel where everyone waits for afternoon tea in gloomy silence. If we went abroad we never flew – it was far too expensive – but usually took a train and carried our own food. One year eight of us, four adults and four children, bundled into a friend's car and set off for the South of France to improve our French. The children did all the shopping and ordering in the cafés and, under my mother's supervision, we did all the budgeting and accounts. We lived on a shoe-string.

Another year we toured Italy in a bus, drinking in the architecture, the museums, the life, and existing on bread and cheese.

I was always encouraged to read on holiday and given books – on shells, if I happened to be collecting them, or on trees if I was making a collage of leaves. I was never condemned to sit alone in a cool, dark room struggling with an essay while everyone else played in the sun, or to grapple with arithmetic to the sound of summer screams and giggles outside. I gained enormously from the calm and lack of pressure and I have always been grateful for the pleasure and wisdom I gained through these holidays.

Even the camping holidays were valuable. Some summers we camped in Wales. There were us four children, my mother, and usually three or four other children whose parents wanted them out of the way – my mother had become a sort of one-woman Dr Barnardo's for the middle classes, adults and children alike, the emotionally halt and the financially lame rushing to be harboured at her hearth. One of these was the dreaded Mr Timing. He was an accountant who looked like a maggot. He had thin, fluffy orange hair and Uriah Heap manners, and he hovered round my mother in over-large shorts and a ridiculous sun hat. We all hated him, but my mother would defend him with: 'Now, Susan, he's very good with figures and knows a lot of Latin.'

Mr Timing did no work, never collected the milk, peeled the potatoes, cleared the plates or emptied the washing-up water. He just made sycophantic compliments to my mother about her cooking, while eating more than his share of the food. (Having cooked for sixty children every day of every term in between giving English lessons and dancing classes, cooking for eight or nine was child's play for my mother.) At night he was too frightened, or too lazy, to cross the field to go to the loo behind a tree, or find and use the billy-can. Instead he would just creep to the other side of the tent. Such behaviour – even to a six-year-old – was repellent. In the morning when my mother asked which child had behaved so disgustingly, Mr Timing would wander away, on the excuse of fetching some Latin poetry to read to my mother.

Looking back, I realize that my mother was always harbouring social misfits and difficult children, children of parents who were getting divorced, or moving to the country. By the time I was ten, one of my sisters, my mother, an American girl, two other English girls and I were all living in our four-roomed flat almost the whole year round. By the time I was fourteen or fifteen, the household had been reduced to my mother, Ann, Suzie Fletcher and me.

Suzie – Susannah York as she is now known – was really luscious. No one could avoid being envious of her. She was extremely voluptuous, always dizzying about in baby-doll nighties. She had a fantastic way of getting everyone to do things for her. Even my mother, who was so busy and had no flies on her, found herself rushing round after Suzie. It is odd that Susannah and I should have known each other so well in our teens; at the time neither of us had any idea that we would both be 'survivors' in show business. On the other hand, perhaps Susannah did have an inkling, since, even then, she was so beautiful. I was only too aware that I was *not* beautiful. I remember making a conscious effort not to keep my head still for too long, hoping, I suppose, that by so doing nobody would notice and comment on my extreme plainness.

Many parents, knowing how exceptionally hard my mother worked, offered to take me off her hands during the holidays as a way of showing their deep gratitude for all that she gave to their children at school. One spring Zita Sutton took her daughter, Maina Gielgud, and me to Opio, a tiny hill village in the South of France. Each morning Zita would drive us down to Cannes for a two-hour ballet lesson with Madame Sèdova, the famous Russian ballet teacher. After the lesson we'd go home to a divine lunch, with plenty of raw garlic for our health, steak for our strength and salad for our skin. Then, with loving patience, Zita would help us to practise most of the afternoon. But, always lurking somewhere inside me, was the knowledge that I was not perfect enough physically to be a classical ballet dancer, though I know of no other form of expression in which one's soul soars to greater heights. The joy of expressing music in movement surpasses all else, but the physical effort needed to keep my technique good enough, to make everything appear easy, was always dragging me down. When, at fifteen, I grew too tall to be a classical ballet dancer, it came as a relief deep inside me, in spite of the fact that my mother sent me to be trained by great teachers all over the world, in Paris, New York and London.

I look back on the holiday with Zita and Maina as very special and, in the nicest way, flash – living in a villa, flying in a plane and lunching in St Paul de Vence with Maina's great-uncle, Gordon Craig, Ellen Terry's son.

Even though Craig must have been in his eighties, the way he looked at me made me aware for the first time that I was a woman. He smiled and patted my bottom and I remember jumping, not knowing quite where to turn, and asking if I could take a photograph of him. He didn't seem to mind, though Zita said later, 'He really doesn't want to see people these days.' I was fascinated by his long white hair, as fine as a baby's, his huge black hat and black cloak. When we said goodbye, he squeezed me again, and again I was aware that there were men in the world as well as girls.

Maina Gielgud moved on and up – despite the fact that she was tall she did not allow this to trouble her. She is now a remarkable dancer with a niche all of her own in the ballet world.

Another friend whose family used to invite me for holidays was Susan Stranks. One Easter we all went to Cromer.

Alan Stranks, Susan's father, was a writer. He always

seemed to be working on his scripts for BBC Radio's *P.C. 49* series, helped by his wife, who did all the typing. But on this particular holiday there was to be no work, just rest.

In one way it was lovely for me to stay with the Stranks: there were never any haunting meal-time questions like, 'What have you two girls learned this term?' In another way it was rather frightening for me because Mr Stranks was very keen on word games. Susan was very good at them, but I, of course, dreaded them and usually found some excuse to avoid them, like offering to sew a missing button back on to Mr Stranks's jacket.

In an antique shop in Cromer High Street there was a tiny engraved silver heart – about half the size of my thumbnail. I wanted it desperately, but it cost over five shillings – way beyond my means. Still, I wanted it, I had to get it – somehow. I noticed that Mr Stranks had another button missing and a jacket elbow that needed darning, so I offered to do them for him, hoping in my heart he'd give me a shilling or so for my efforts. But after I had meticulously finished darning and sewing on the button and presented the work to him he thanked me, touched my hair, smiled, and said, 'You'll be rewarded in Heaven.'

I didn't want to be rewarded in Heaven. I wanted to be rewarded *now*. I felt all watery, I wanted the heart so much. Every time I passed the shop it was agony. I could see that the heart was still in the window – but would it be there tomorrow? I was sure someone else would want to buy such a perfect thing.

The days passed, and the heart became the most important object and thought in my life. Who would own it by the time I was twenty and could afford to buy it? Would I ever see it again? Each day we walked by the shop I could see it, still there, glowing on its black velvet pad. But on the last day I saw it was gone. Someone else had bought it. It would never be mine. I was never a crier – but I wished I could cry. I did not.

In the car on the way back to London, Alan Stranks said to his wife, 'How much pocket money are the girls owed?'

'Oh, about a week or so', Mrs Stranks replied.

Mr Stranks tossed two little packets from his pocket into the back of the car.

'There you are, something each.' In my little crumpled packet was the silver heart.

Curiously enough, many holidays were spent with my mother's other star pupils, Anthony and Carole Dowell, my adored friends. At school, when the bell went for the daily walk in the park and we all formed a crocodile, everyone rushed to hold hands with the two Dowells. Both Carole and Anthony were warm, gentle creatures, who accepted their popularity so easily and naturally that no one ever resented their position. Even in the dancing-class the fact that they were always praised and asked to do their *grand jetés* alone for us all to watch, never caused jealousy.

My mother felt in her bones that Anthony had the making of a great dancer when he was six, and persuaded his mother to let him audition for the Royal Ballet School. He shone like a star from the word go. In school concerts he exuded a magic musicality and brilliance, and in class he was technically superb for his age, instinctively understanding the roots of ballet. It is so sad that my mother did not live to see him achieve the heights she always predicted.

Anthony had so many other gifts, drawing, painting, puppetry (his passion), paper-sculpture, tap-dancing, musical comedy, singing. No wonder we all admired him so much and wanted to hold his hand in the park. We all took graciously the fact that he often teamed up with Anthony Elliott, who now runs *Time Out*. Anthony Dowell was several years younger than me but, if children can be in love, I certainly loved him, with a silent longing to be near this divine creature who did everything that was important to me so well. With the Dowell family I went to South Devon, to a little bungalow on the edge of a great wide sandy cove. We came home calm, happy and wonderfully brown.

49

A little paper pop-up Anthony made for me when he was only six or seven years old is the only theatrical mascot I have. It is permanently in my make-up box, and I take it with me from theatre to theatre. One night when I was doing a Charity Gala I forgot the pop-up. By a strange coincidence the Gala was 'An Evening with Anthony Dowell' and so there I was, working with him, but without my treasured mascot. I had rushed to the theatre from rehearsing another play on the far side of London and I'd asked myself, 'Have I left anything behind, anything I should have with me?' I hadn't been able to think of a thing.

I went on stage, nerves moderately under control, voice there, legs not visibly shaking and started the song that Bert Shevelove had written specially for the occasion. The words flowed out, I managed to remember the extremely complicated and very witty lyrics, and the audience laughed in all the right places. I got to the end of the first chorus, then the second, then, in the third and last verse, I froze. I couldn't remember the next line, and instead of making something up I said, 'I can't remember what comes next.' This was something that had never happened to me before. I recovered quickly and carried on with the song, but when I got back to my dressing-room, I was shaking and sweating. I immediately went through my things, to see if my mascot was anywhere to be found and it was not. I knew I should never leave it behind again.

6

BY THE time I was ten, I was so used to academic failure that it had ceased to trouble me, or so I must assume since I have no memory of being troubled at that age. Only later did a feeling of complete helplessness overcome me. I can remember that, though until now I have never admitted it, even to myself.

My family continued to cover up for me and help me as much as they could. Jane and Ann would buy picture books, designed for a younger age group, to encourage me to read, but usually I persuaded them to read to me. I remember *Susan Swan,* the story of a little girl who, abandoned by her parents, makes friends with a swan who protects her, feeds her and eventually lets her live with the swan family on the river bank. Ann must have read me the book fifty times, and I sat behind her and silently cried fifty times. Yet even if I knew a book backwards, to read it for myself was still arduous. The words never looked the same. Suddenly I'd think, 'I've never seen this page before. I don't recognize these words.' What made it worse was that on a 'good day', when all the messages from eyes, ears and mouth were working simultaneously, I could read, say *Pride and Prejudice,* with comparative ease.

The 'good days' syndrome started very early on. The 'strings' from eyes, ears and mouth to hands worked; in reading and writing there was no confusion of message or

LEFT SIDE

Patterns

The left side of the brain tends to govern spontaneous and emotional concepts, and ideas concerning space and shape.

RIGHT SIDE

Linear

The right side of the brain tends to govern sequential and logical concepts, including language.

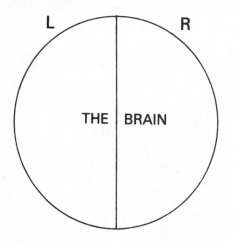

The left side of the brain has a tendency to control the right-hand field of vision and body mechanism.

The right side of the brain has a tendency to control the left-hand field of vision and body mechanism.

communication up and down the line. So b's were not mistaken for d's or p's for g's and everything flowed. I had no idea, of course, that the brain worked in a mysterious way, with the right side governing the left side of the body and the left governing the right, or that my own brain was working in reverse.

The brain seems to mature in sudden stages. There is often a jump at the age of nine, and again at eleven. My mother was convinced that, for me, the great leap would come at thirteen or fourteen.

'At thirteen or fourteen your mind will suddenly develop,' she would say – so often that it became a kind of catechism. 'You will find work very easy and academically you will make great strides. You're a late developer, that's all. It's very common. Always think of that when you don't find things easy. Just think, at thirteen all will be well.'

At thirteen all was not well. But 'late developer' sounded like a good phrase and I clung on to it. In the meantime my only real access to the joy of books was through my schoolfriends. I had five or six friends who were good readers, who enjoyed reading aloud, and who were prepared to share with me what was to them the easiest thing in the world – reading.

Patricia Beckwith could read Charles Dickens or the Brönte sisters aloud, without any signs of fatigue, for as much as three or four hours at a time. I listened enraptured, drinking in the tale, but never for a moment questioning why I wasn't reading it myself. Good readers read and good listeners listen. I was a listener.

Some of my younger friends, like Jane Beyfus, managed not to read to me at all, but asked their nannies to read to us instead. Then we would act out the book for the nanny and the parents in the drawing-room after tea. I enjoyed this enormously – acting a book instead of reading it – and it gave me what I suppose must have been my second taste of success, of applause, of people appreciating me. The first taste had occurred when I was very young.

My mother and I were travelling on the Underground one day when my mother recognized a friend of hers, who was in some way connected with the film business, and happened to be looking for a child to play Jean Simmons as a little girl in a film called *Woman in the Hall*. I went to the studios, tested, and got the part. I was paid £50 for three weeks' work and it was almost the ruin of me, so dreadfully was I spoiled. I was driven to work early in the morning in a luxuriously warm car. Just hearing people shouting 'Action!' and 'Cut!', just that little taste of what filming was all about, meant that I longed for the day when I would be grown up and could get back to that exhilarating ambience.

I adored every minute of it. Jean Simmons was a big star but she was always very sweet to me when she came onto the set. I also became devoted to Ursula Jeans, who played my mother in the film, and wanted her to adopt me – much to my own mother's horror. Ursula had no children of her own and she promised to take me to the Zoo when my work in the film was over.

I told all my school friends, 'I won't be having lunch with you today. A film star is coming to take me out.'

I waited downstairs in my Harris tweed coat – and waited and waited. After four hours there was still no sign of Ursula. My mother kept saying, 'This is ridiculous, Susan. You're freezing cold. You must come upstairs and have school lunch.'

Ursula never did arrive, and later I heard the explanation. She had been called in to do more filming and had sent a telegram which had been delivered to the wrong address. So we never went to the Zoo together. She was very kind to me all the same. At the end of the filming she gave me a huge teddy bear, called Mr Bruno, which had featured in the film.

The feeling of achievement that other school children got from getting high marks, or a good report, I got from this film. Acting for Jane Beyfus's parents gave me the same feeling. They smiled and laughed, and I felt fulfilled.

At the same time, since both radio and television were not allowed in the house (my mother thought they would 'soggy the mind'), and the world of books was closed to me, another world opened up – my own. I wrote copiously, a page a day in my diary, many long letters, never posted, and endless monologues and playlets. I was happy to write so much because what I wrote was secret. No one would ever see it. So no one could ever check my spelling.

The playlets were usually monologues about a deranged farm girl in Eastern Europe, who was cold and hungry, having been cast out into the fields! I acted them in my room for hours on end. I would crouch, clutching an imaginary shawl round my shoulders, and declaim, 'Don't leave me, at this hour when I am so weak and lonely. Help me to stand so I can see the light through the barn door before you leave me . . . and I leave you . . . for ever' and so on.

The interest for me was not so much in the writing or the acting as in fantasy itself. It was extremely therapeutic, especially when the play was really gruesome, and the character had only one eye, one arm, and one leg, and could hardly talk. (I've hankered after that sort of part for the rest of my life.) Later the parts graduated to a mad, pregnant village girl who found it hard to understand how she had conceived. With my clothes hitched up and my hair hanging over my face, leaning against the wall I'd ask: 'How can this be? I am so heavy and my belly weighs me down. Is it something I have eaten? Yet I have not eaten for days. Something is growing inside me. I feel it move, as though I have eaten a live rabbit that is trying to get out. Someone help me open the prison door.'

It was hardly surprising that I should have had this naive view of pregnancy, since our sex education had consisted of being told, 'A seed flies across the room from the man to the woman.' My anxiety was always, if there happened to be two women in a room, which one would get the seed?

For a woman as intelligent as my mother to fill us with, 'Sex is wicked,' 'Never look at someone without their clothes on,' and 'Don't show your body,' was amazing. In fact, the rudest word I knew until I was almost fourteen was 'body' – I thought it was wicked. Luckily my eldest sister, Jane, who encouraged my acting and writing so much, set a good example and when I was in my early teens married and had three children. She told me: 'Don't believe everything Mummy tells you about men.'

* * *

In the 1950s young girls leaving school had many more options open to them than just preparing themselves for marriage. The universities, medical schools, hospitals and law schools were taking a small percentage of women who had their hearts set on better things than being legally made an unpaid housekeeper. But what were the options open to me?

My two older sisters had worked for a short time in the theatre and now taught in the school. This, of course, I could not do. I still had not mastered the alphabet. I didn't get any 'O' levels, except Art, as I couldn't read the questions – the type was too small. (I'd given up, doodled on the examination paper and scribbled a short note to the examiner, protesting that the questions were incomprehensible.) Latin, the most important subject in my mother's eyes, I did not even attempt to take. What path could possibly be open to a girl with my remarkable lack of achievement? Mother's help? Cook? Children's nanny? Gardener? Swimming pool attendant? I couldn't even become a chauffeuse – I didn't know right from left – or a telephonist, since I couldn't remember numbers in sequence. I couldn't become a nurse as Latin 'O' level was obligatory, nor a secretary since I couldn't spell and shorthand was even more mysterious to me than plain English. I thought of modelling but assumed that to succeed I would have to be much prettier and with smaller hips. The answer seemed to be marriage. Yet it was a solution I could not accept. It meant loss of freedom and freedom was a very high priority.

If I had known what was the matter with me and why I couldn't read, would everything have been easier just because my difficulties had a name? Yes, it would. Perhaps the need to survive would not have been so strong, perhaps I would not have been so resilient, but it would have been easier, just knowing that I was not mentally retarded, or lazy, or backward, or emotionally disturbed, but that the small part of my brain governing language was not functioning, either through heredity, or conditions at birth, and that the malfunction had a NAME. To know that it was not a disease but a disability, a condition that could be improved, would have made all the difference.

Nevertheless, even with my nameless disability, things were on my side. I had been to my mother's school, protected and encouraged, and without this approach, the reading and spelling problems would have over-ridden all else. But they hadn't.

I felt that there must be some avenue of employment open to me and it was up to me to find it. I remembered the sense of achievement I had felt when filming as a child, I remembered the first laugh I had got at a school concert, and acting for Jane Beyfus's parents. I told myself that I was alive, in good health, optimistic, a reasonable looker (although I felt extremely ugly) and was, in fact, surrounded by advantages. And then Fate, in the form of my father, gave me the final push. One day, when I was fifteen, I asked him, 'Daddy will you lend me a pound to buy some stockings?'

He answered, 'I earn my living, you earn yours.'

He meant it.

I earned it.

I sat down, and with the help of Jane's husband, Chris, wrote a hundred letters to all the repertory companies in England. I got one reply, with the offer of a job.

7

WHO WOULD have thought that joining one of Frank H. Fortescue's Companies, at the Roof Garden Theatre, Bognor Regis, as assistant stage manager (and small parts) at £6-10s a week would mean having to read so much? An actress, I had assumed, has to act, but not read endlessly.

Every eight days we performed a new play. The choice was governed by the fact that our director, Walter Claybourne, and his wife had played the parts every season for the last two decades. Every play had to have a part for a woman over forty, and another for a man in his fifties. As the assistant stage manager taking small parts when required, I played whatever parts were left, even the roles of boys.

The first part I was given was Dora in Emlyn Williams' *Night Must Fall*, the story of a psychopathic killer called Danny, who goes to work for a Mrs Bramson, an old lady in a wheel chair who lives in a deserted cottage with her niece, Olivia, and her maid, Dora.

It was lucky for me that this should be my first part, as I had been introduced to the play by the author himself. Brook Williams, Emlyn Williams' youngest son, had been my childhood sweetheart, and I'd spent a lot of time at their house. Sometimes Emlyn would ask me to hear his lines for his one-man show, *Dylan Thomas*. I always agreed, but secretly I prayed he wouldn't dry for I should never have been able to help him. I followed the script with my finger and, if he did stop, I'd say, 'I can't read this bit – the typing is a bit faint'. He'd glance at it and carry on. I was so grateful that he didn't comment on my apparent blindness; the typing was, in fact, perfectly clear. Observing his dedication to work, and the wonderfully interesting life that the Williams family led, had been another incentive to me, in becoming an actress. Yet at their smart parties, with everyone from Laurence Olivier to Terence Rattigan there, I would stay in the kitchen most of the time and talk to their Yorkshire cook, lest anyone asked me how I'd done in my O-levels and what book I was reading.

In *Night Must Fall* the director's wife, Mrs Claybourne, always played Mrs Bramson, and Mr Claybourne, being in the older age group, refrained from playing Danny and played the Police Inspector instead. At rehearsals Mrs Claybourne would say, 'You go down there, dear, where I can see you. That's where the girl who plays Dora usually goes.'

At sixteen there are no rules, especially if one hasn't been to drama school, so being down stage, in the dark, didn't seem odd, or worry me at all, until the first night, when I simply moved up stage and into the light. In the interval Mrs Claybourne took me aside and said, 'What on earth did you do that for, dear? Change your position like that?'

'Well, Mrs Claybourne, the audience couldn't see me where I was and I thought they should.'

The arrogance of sixteen! If only I had retained it!

Every Tuesday for the next six months I had to read aloud with the other members of the cast the play we were about to rehearse. Virtually every Tuesday morning of those six months, at the first reading, I could not and did not read but made up most of the part. As it is common for actors to be hesitant at the first reading of a play, my complete incompetence at the read-through was put down to nerves, and my ad-libs to fear.

But perhaps a third of the way through the reading, if I had a fairly large part, Mr Claybourne, who was not only the director but actor-manager as well, would ask me to make the tea, then hastily read my part for me, often shouting at me in front of the Company as I left: 'You'd be a lot better actress if you weren't a virgin'. (I'd have been a lot better actress if I had been able to read.)

But *still* I did not admit I could not read fluently. I developed all sorts of techniques to cover up my disability: spilling my tea during a long speech; pretending to have a bad cold, blowing my nose and talking from behind my hanky; complaining of period pains or simply going to the lavatory; affecting to be too hot, and taking my cardigan off, or too cold and having to fetch a coat; marking my speeches with a pencil. Mr Claybourne must have been very kind, or very hard-pressed to find a replacement, not to have sacked me. If he had, I would have wondered why – I was doing my best!

During the day there were rehearsals and general A.S.M. donkey work. In the evening there was a play to perform. At night I sat up to all hours trying to read the next play, or to learn the one we were rehearsing. Learning my lines in those early days, when my brain was not trained and disciplined as it is now, was nerve-racking and exhausting. I always felt that I would never manage to master the lines in time. I used to learn a rough approximation of the text by sitting up all night, repeating the lines to myself over and over again, without really thinking about what I was saying. During the day I would go over my lines with anyone who was prepared to hear them; in fact I would see people only on condition that they heard my lines. Nothing but work mattered. Going out, conversation – unless it was to do with the play – eating, boyfriends, were all totally unimportant to me. Only the work existed. Much later, through dedicated application, I trained myself to study plays comparatively quickly, to read them with understanding, learn parts through their meaning and not like a parrot, and read books which threw light on the subject of the play, its period, or characters. But at Bognor simply the achieve-

60

*My mother as a pupil
at dancing school*

*My father as an
undergraduate at Oxford*

My sisters, Jane and Ann, dressed for a school dancing display

My brother John and I, with our father

With my brother and sisters, working on our kitchen garden

Seeing John, Jane and Ann off to school at the end of the war

One of my mother's early dancing classes

Mrs Hampshire's School group in Hyde Park. I'm in the back row, second from the left

Writing lessons with Jane. My Aunt Dora said recently, 'There was nothing wrong with your brain – your sister Jane used to teach you.'

Rehearsing at St Saviours Church Hall, with Kathleen Keep at the piano

Photograph Jason Shenai

Anthony Dowell with Jane Beyfus

The paper keepsake that Anthony made for me – now my priceless mascot. On it he wrote, 'To Darling Susie, with millions of kisses and good luck.'

On our way to a school concert, with Anthony in the front row, and me at the back

Maina Gielgud and I with Madame Sèdova in the South of France, during our daily lessons in Cannes

Gordon Craig, Zita Sutton and her husband, Colonel Sutton, and their daughter, Maina Gielgud. The photograph was taken by me while we were visiting St Paul de Vence

Two of my early stage
performances at school.
Left: *playing a maid at the
Fortune Theatre with Carol
Dowell.* Below: *a school
play with Susan Stranks*

ment of learning lines was far more important to me than their meaning. In any case, as my vocabulary was so small, I didn't know what half the words meant.

I was appallingly bad in almost every play we did that first season. I resorted to 'corpsing', trying to look pretty, using charm (whatever I thought that was) and smiling at the audience, even adding a joke, if I thought they liked me. Once, when I had to eat a piece of bread in some scene, and didn't manage to swallow in time for my next line, I turned to the audience, with my mouth full, and said, 'I've got to finish it, it's free.'

Of course, I had no business at all to go out of character and leave my fellow actor waiting for his cue while I finished my mouthful and chatted to the audience, but I did – I thought it was acting. Members of the audience could be heard complaining, when leaving, 'She doesn't take her part well, does she?' I'd see the same old faces back the following week to see if I'd got any better. I hadn't.

The tasks of an Assistant Stage Manager are those of a general dog's body and a wonderful introduction to working in the theatre. I had not been to a drama school, as my decision to become an actress had been so sudden that there had been no time to apply, and probably still less chance of being accepted, but in any case my experience at school had taught me that I learned best by absorbing things through experience, and so Mr and Mrs Claybourne's company was a perfect training-ground for me.

I never remember being so happy. I was earning my own living, I went everywhere on a bicycle, I even had money to spare: my salary was £6-10s a week, my digs £2-15s. I realize now I must have been the most appalling actress, but I had no responsibility, nothing to live up to, so it didn't really matter to me if the local press said I wasn't much to write home about – I didn't read the papers anyway. I sometimes pine for that feeling of freedom, the carefree happiness that goes with innocence and lack of responsibility.

Even the chores I had to do as A.S.M. were bliss: sweeping the stage, making the tea, running errands, buying Woodbines for the cast, arranging chairs in a semi-circle and putting ash-trays on the tables before a read-through, making sure that I collected props, and all the actors had their personal props. It was my job to set the stage so the furniture was in the correct position and change the set from one scene to another. In small, unsubsidized companies it was not uncommon for the A.S.M. to help make and paint the scenery, and this I often did. I would make props too, or borrow any unusual item required, like a cat or a dog. When I was not on stage myself (wearing the thickest make-up imaginable) I was in charge of the lights, tabs,* music and grams.† It was not unusual for me to come off stage, make a dash for the curtains, pull them down, bring up the front of the house lights and the music for the interval. At the beginning of the next act I'd reverse the process and then appear on stage, panting and exhilarated, to start the next scene.

If the day had had a thousand hours and I had been asked to make a thousand more cups of tea, or a thousand more props, still I would never have tired. For the first time in my life I felt that I was in control, and I have never really known a feeling like it since. It was my first taste of living without being questioned. How do you spell 'incredible'? What's the square root of ninety-four? Which continent produces the most wheat? It seemed as though none of that mattered any more.

The summer season at Bognor came to an end and I had to cast around for another job. I was lucky enough to be offered a position at the Oxford Playhouse as a student A.S.M. at £1-5s a week. The plays they performed at Oxford were mainly the classics, and a far cry from the lightweight pieces put on to entertain the holiday-makers of Bognor, so I considered this new job to be a real step up.

* Curtains.
† Gramophones.

The meagre pay was subsidized by my father (bless his Yorkshire heart) to the tune of £2 a week, plus the £1 a week profit I made on providing the cast with tea and the odd bit of washing, for 10s or so. I managed to survive quite happily on about £5 a week, doing very little acting and eating raw carrots, bread, and liver and eggs cooked in the theatre, and paying £2-10s for my digs, bed and breakfast and cold evening meal, if desired!

When I left the Oxford Playhouse six months later I was remembered for only one thing: never completing the painting of the front-of-house lavatory. I was asked to do it, and started, but then, because I was such a willing soul, if I was asked to make the curtains for the next production, and on top of that to dye all the sandals brown for a new play, I'd say 'yes'. The result was that the lavatory remained half-painted, a fact of which I am reminded, much to my annoyance, by everyone who has worked at the Oxford Playhouse.

But I do think, with all due modesty, that a well-known actor who had better remain nameless may also remember me, or anyway the A.S.M. who was 'on the book', prompting the play in which he was starring. The irony that I of all people should be asked to prompt need not be stressed.

To make matters worse, the play was an English translation of a Greek tragedy with a complex and difficult text. Although, had it been Punch and Judy, my efficiency as a prompter would have been equally lamentable.

Sure enough, when the actor dried he waited for me to give him the next line. Thinking that this was an 'actor's pause', for dramatic effect, I looked at him and waited. Silence. Eventually he whispered desperately, 'Line.'

'Line?'

'Yes. Line. Prompt.'

Ah yes, the prompt. But I could not give him the prompt because not only could I not read the next line on the page, or recognize the last line he had said, I was not even sure that I was on the right page. Eventually he broke the terrible silence again by repeating his last line, and idiotically I said it back to him! He turned away and groaned as if it were part of the performance, and raised his eyes to the heavens, while I frantically tried to find the place in the script, praying that, as so often happens, one of the other actors on the stage would help him out.

But there was only one other character on stage – his mother – and she was supposed to be dead.

Sweat was pouring off me like ten dripping taps, I was blind with fear. My helpless victim hissed at me again, 'Prompt! Prompt!' and again he repeated his last line and again I said it back to him. Then suddenly I saw a line I could read. I could read it because it was a short line, on its own, not part of a long speech. Unfortunately it was one of the mother's lines. But I said it, 'Oh my son!'

Nothing happened. I said it again.

'Oh my son!'

In total panic I started to turn the pages, blurting out at random any line I recognized. In despair the actor started to walk towards the prompt corner. At the same time I heard the footsteps of the company manager racing up from the auditorium.

As the actor reached the prompt corner, and the company manager arrived backstage and grabbed the script from me, the voice of the director was heard from the stalls shouting out the line at last, and then moaning, 'Oh , my God!'

*　　*　　*

In those early days I was an avid reader of theatrical textbooks, short, simple treatises on the art of make-up, or dress-making for beginners, or any little book which was not too long and which would help me in my work. The fact that I totally misunderstood half of them came to light one night after an Oxford Playhouse performance of *The Heartless Princess,* when a friend visited me backstage.

'Susan, it was lovely,' she said, 'but from the front you

look as if you've dipped your nose in a bag of flour.'

I couldn't believe my ears. I rather prided myself on my make-up – if not my acting.

'What d'you mean?' I protested.

'You look as if your nose has been dipped in flour,' she repeated.

'I don't believe you. It can't. I've made up this way for nine months and no one's ever mentioned it before.'

My friend went quiet. Eventually she said, 'Well, it still looks very odd.'

Something in her tone of voice made me rush to a mirror. I studied my face. My nose looked perfectly all right to me – white at the end and shaded all round, just as the book had suggested.

'I'll show you my make-up book,' I said, and we went to my skip and I found the book. But the stage doorkeeper was waiting to close the theatre, so I invited my friend to have supper at my digs so that we could study the book together. We leafed through the book while consuming my landlady's sweatiest cold ham with beetroot in vinegar.

'Here you are,' I said as I found the right page. I picked my way through the words and began to feel profoundly silly. 'I think I may have misread it,' I said. My friend took the book and glanced at it. 'I think you may have,' she said drily. 'It's a white line down the *bridge* of the nose and a little shading under it. All the difference in the world.'

'But I've done fifteen plays with white on the end of my nose!'

'Then you've done fifteen plays looking as if your nose has been dipped in flour. You should read more carefully in future.'

I asked her to read it *all* to me, as I was sure I had misunderstood the whole section on juvenile make-up.

No wonder they laughed at me in Bognor!

8

AFTER MY short but happy stint at the Oxford Playhouse I went back to London and began auditioning almost daily, with every hope that the next audition would turn me into a star! But two years and what now seems like a thousand auditions later, I was still an A.S.M., although I had at least learned a few tricks about how to cover up my reading difficulties.

When, as so often happened, an audition was interrupted by a shout from the stalls, 'Stick to the text – this isn't a play-writing competition,' I would nip down off the stage, frilly skirt flying, and plead quietly with the stage manager or the director, 'Can I take the script away for an hour? I can't see very well – bad eyes. I'll study it and try again later.'

About one in every eight of such attempts succeeded.

'Oh, all right. Come back in an hour.'

On my return, I would read the part with a stammer, as though the character was very shy and vulnerable. This apprehensive style stood me in good stead through many an audition, and was termed 'sensitive acting'.

A second dodge was to concentrate on singing auditions rather than reading ones. Thus, many of my early jobs turned out to be in musicals.

Another technique by which I avoided reading altogether was to offer to do 'a little piece I've written myself'. I was completely oblivious to the absurdity of an aspiring actress portraying a deaf, crippled, pregnant, starving peasant girl begging a farmer not to take away the pet goat that was her only friend. Only too often I was asked to perform this grim monologue again – when a director had mustered some of his friends. But the repeat performance never resulted in a job – I could never think why! It had seemed fine when I'd done it in my bedroom at the age of fifteen. Why had it not matured in the three-year interval? Surely John Dexter, auditioning me for the Royal Court, would see some merit in it? He did not.

One sunny Wednesday I was waiting at the stage door of the Wyndhams Theatre for my turn to audition and chatting to the doorkeeper.

'What do you think then?' the doorkeeper asked, leaning out of his window. 'What are your chances?'

'Well, I don't think I'll get it. I don't seem to read well at auditions.'

He looked at me.

'You're probably nervous. Do you never work then?'

'Oh yes, I'm very lucky. I'm nearly always employed. I'm round the corner in Leicester Square at the Arts Theatre as an A.S.M. They let me off for auditions. I expect they get a bit fed up as I seem to go to one or two a day.'

'Well, if you're going to that many and you're not getting the jobs – a girl with a nice personality like you – you're either no good, or you're not lucky.'

That's it, I thought! I'm just not lucky.

When I got back to the Arts Theatre, having, needless to say, failed the audition, I set about my menial tasks, cleaning up the stage, and preparing the props for the evening's show. But the usual cheerful song was not on my lips. One of the stage hands noticed my gloom.

'What's up then? You're not your usual chirpy self,' he said.

I found myself suddenly pouring out my heart. I told him about the endless auditions, how I never got the job, how I was desperate, how I felt sure that the other actresses weren't so much better than me, or any more right for a part, yet they always got the work. I told him that I found reading at auditions almost impossible as I was so nervous and couldn't see the words, or make much sense of a part when sight-reading.

'I think I'll go on failing auditions for the rest of my life,' I sighed, tears welling in my eyes.

I don't remember the name of the stage hand I was talking to, but I remember *him*, for he was to give me the first glimmer of hope in my working life.

He told me that he had a younger brother who was pretty bright but who also had difficulty in reading. They had an aunt in America who had told them that the name for this difficulty was 'word blindness'. 'Perhaps,' he suggested, 'you've got the same trouble – word blindness.'

This little phrase, 'word blindness', changed my life. It gave me a 'hook' to hang my trouble on. It was a phrase I could use as a cover for the problem I couldn't understand.

'Word blindness.' A wonderful phrase. It kept running through my head. I thought, Susan, all you've got to tell people is, 'I suffer from word blindness,' and that will explain everything.

In fact, I didn't have to use the phrase for some time, as Oscar Lewenstein and Wolf Mankowitz, my bosses at the Arts Theatre, were casting *Expresso Bongo*, a new musical written by Wolf and starring Paul Scofield, and I was allowed to audition. As I explained earlier, singing auditions were always easier for me. I auditioned along with hundreds of other girls, and got a job. Alas, yet again it was as an A.S.M. and understudy, but still there was the prospect of a ten-week tour of the provinces and then the West End, at the old Saville Theatre. I would be able to live at home – and keep auditioning!

Rehearsals moved into their fourth week. I was very happy making the tea and running errands, and I was earning good money – £12-10s a week. One or two of the smaller female parts still weren't cast, and it seemed possible that they might go to members of the cast if we didn't have further auditions soon. Stage managers usually 'read in' for anyone not cast or missing. In our show the cast was getting a bit fed up with a thirty-five-year-old man trying to pretend he was an eighteen-year-old debutante, so I was asked to read in for the time being. I knew the script pretty well and therefore I was not frightened. In fact, I found it all very exciting. Oscar Lewenstein would pace up and down the stalls with Wolf Mankowitz whispering softly about what was happening on stage in true Hollywood movie style And, again in Hollywood style, some three days later, out of the blue, I was told that I was going to play the part of the debutante. It was the break for which I had been waiting so long.

Curiously enough, I had actually been a real-life debutante for a very brief, unhappy period. At the time when I had been tentatively finding my feet in the theatrical world of Brook Williams' house, my mother had decided to launch me in a conventional debutante fashion. There was absolutely nothing of the conventional deb' about me: I wasn't rich and I rode to most dances on my bicycle.

A friend of my mother agreed to present me at Court, so we went to Buckingham Palace together. We climbed endless flights of stairs, passed from one gold room to another, along with two thousand other girls in silk frocks and flowered hats. Eventually I was presented – all I can remember about it was how clumsily most people curtsied, for lunch and the Queen and I were the only ladies present.

I thought how much I'd rather have been visiting the Palace for the right reason, and not just because my parents hadn't been divorced and had put my name on the list. The right reason came many years later, in 1976, after the 'Pallisers'. At that occasion there were only six or eight guests for lunch and the Queen and I were the only ladies present.

As a debutante, I suppose I was never really more than an outsider, an observer looking on. I didn't finish the

Season, and cancelled my coming-out dance.

* * *

But now, with a part in *Expresso Bongo*, my life seemed at last to be going the right way. There was no increase in wages, but my name would be on the posters and it would be my first West End appearance. Making tea had got me a long way. I had only six or eight lines, but they happened to be extremely funny and very topical. They 'stopped the show' on the first night in London, and Harold Hobson gave me a mention in *The Sunday Times*. Paul Scofield teased me. 'We do all the work,' he said, 'and *The Sunday Times* says things like "the West End should see more of Susan Hampshire". Is it fair?'

At least I had the sense to realize that I had got the part – and my first real break – precisely because I had not had to read for it. I knew that if I had to read for my next part, the chances of 'the West End seeing more of Susan Hampshire' would be remote.

And so it proved. After *Expresso Bongo*'s year-long run was over, I was back to auditioning again. I found that the magical new cover-up phrase, 'word blindness', made not the slightest difference. Once again auditions were dominated by my stupidly unpredictable reading, and the only parts I got were those for which I *looked* right. Interesting work I could not get without doing a good reading, so a great spate of mediocre parts engulfed me, and only occasionally did I do anything of which I could be proud. Producers and directors would say, 'In so many ways you're right for the part – but your reading . . . we can't take the risk.'

The major problem about 'resting' in between acting jobs is keeping alive, finding enough money for food, rent, clothes, Equity dues, singing, dancing, and voice lessons. So, when a friend of mine got me a job as compère for a knitwear fashion show for six weeks I leapt at the opportunity. The salary seemed staggering – £60 a week – and all I had to do was to sit at a desk, with a spotlight on me, and read descriptions of the knitwear being modelled, while buyers from the big department stores sat round the room on gilt chairs, marking their cards and jotting down their orders. Even though I had admitted to myself that I was 'word blind' and faced the fact that I was a hopeless reader, I accepted the job.

On the first morning I was handed twenty closely typed pages of commentary. I took the thick wad of paper and hastily said that I would retire to the cloakroom to study them. I was in a panic. Twenty pages of words that I had never seen before? What was I to do? I must have been mad. I quickly got out a pencil and started to underline what I thought were the key words – 'cardigan', 'jumper', the colours, and so forth. At the end of each descriptive passage there were little jokes and witty comments. These I ringed, feeling that if the worse came to the worst, I could leave them out. It seemed to me that the descriptions were the important things. There were a mass of reference numbers and wholesale prices which didn't seem in the least important to me so I didn't bother to underline them, never realizing that they constituted the most vital information of all as far as the buyers were concerned.

I came out of the cloakroom to find the showroom hushed. Soft music was playing. Good, I thought, music; no one will be able to hear me anyway. I sat down at my desk and the spotlight was turned on me. Damn, I thought, they'll all be able to see me. Then lights hit the centre of the showroom floor, where the models were going to parade and I received the signal to start my welcoming speech.

It was a nice, simple sentence:

'Good morning, ladies, and welcome to Braemar's Spring Collection'.

What I actually said was, 'Good morning, ladies and gentlemen (some laughter since there were no men present), I hope you enjoy the collection. Oh yes – it's boring . . . er,

71

I mean Braemar'. (A few coughs and one clap.)

Why I said 'boring' instead of 'Braemar' I shall never know. It was probably nerves.

The chief designer nipped over to my desk to check that I had the right bits of paper. 'Don't worry,' I said. 'All I need is a cup of coffee – and my glasses.' She rushed back with a magnifying glass. 'I'll be fine,' I reassured her, holding the papers close to my eyes and pretending to squint. I began to read.

'Number one – sorry – our first number is a B deck sweat in Peru. No, sorry, a V neck sweater in blue.'

There were titters; and the chief designer rushed over again. She snapped her fingers and a cup of coffee materialized. I continued.

'This beautifully soft jumper in push cashmere has tribbed tuffs – I mean ribbed cuffs – and is both sparky and tart – er, smart and sporty.'

Mistake after mistake. By now the models were convulsed; the buyers were confused and amazed. I kept reversing the digits in the prices and reference numbers. They had never heard anything like it.

By the end of that first morning I knew the only thing I could possibly do was to resign before they fired me. So I went to the office and, full of shame, offered my resignation. I confronted a well-dressed, well-built lady.

'Nonsense,' she said. 'I hear the show was a great success. Memorable, in fact. All the buyers are commenting on it. Tomorrow just give it a little more of your own personality. Oh – and try to get at least some of the prices right.'

I backed out of the office in utter confusion and took the script home to study it. The following morning I arrived at work full of hope and happiness. I managed to give a thoroughly reliable reading and no one laughed. I felt relieved and pleased with myself. My hard work overnight had paid off. I went to the office for a cup of coffee, rather hoping that people would congratulate me.

Suddenly I heard the well-dressed woman's voice.

'Try to keep it fresh, dear,' she said. 'Like you did it yesterday. It's much more amusing that way.'

My mouth dropped open. Did she mean that I should keep in all the mistakes? Surely it was important to get colours and prices right – or did the buyers just want to be amused?

Baffled, I crossed Regent Street and walked down Conduit Street, asking myself what it was they really wanted. In Bond Street I stopped in my tracks and started to retrace my steps back to the showroom, determined to find out the answer. When I arrived everyone had gone to lunch except a young secretary and a house model, who was sitting on a chair in the deserted salon, eating an apple.

'I came back to find out what they meant about the commentary,' I said.

The model took a bite of her apple.

'Just give them a laugh, dear. That's what they want. But there's no need to go over the top like you did yesterday. B deck sweat. Really!'

I went out into the street more bewildered than ever. I couldn't understand how they did not realize that 'B deck sweat' was a mistake.

In the next six weeks I certainly kept the buyers laughing – and I didn't get the sack. On my last morning I understood why. I overheard a voice saying to one of the buyers:

'We used her because she was rather a famous deb'.'

Although it seems hard to believe, even Ros Chatto, my agent since the early 1960s, did not know about my reading problem. When I asked to see a script before an audition she'd say, 'Why on earth do you want the script now? It may well be changed.'

'But, Ros, I must see it,' I'd say. 'Just let me see it.' I couldn't let her know why – I was too ashamed – so I just kept insisting, to her puzzlement.

'Really, Susan, it's not necessary – take my word for it, the part is good. You'll see it at the audition.'

She must have thought it odd that when it came to the

contracts I would not even read them through. I'd just say, 'You check it. How long? What's the money? Any billing? I expect it'll be all right.'

I had to sign contracts, of course, but even that was painful as I was never quite sure what was in them.

The irony is that the actor who reads well is not necessarily the actor who gives the best performance. His best performance may be at the first read-through.

After quite a lot of unmemorable television work, in 1960 I got my first West End starring role in Julian Slade's musical *Follow That Girl*. How I got the part is a minor miracle. The audition was held at the producer Geoffrey Russell's house and it was the very first occasion on which I used my new magic phrase, 'word blindness', and apparently I refused either to read or sing

Julian Slade, the author and composer of the show, and at that time quite one of the most celebrated figures in the British theatre, told me recently, 'We discovered very quickly that you couldn't read. You said you were word blind, or something. But all we were concerned about was the love scene. It was vital. We had to be sure that you could do it. So I didn't want to force you. I think you managed a little sort of reading – to give us an idea – but basically we gave you the part because you were so right for it.'

'But, Julian, didn't I even sing?'

'No. You didn't want to. And I didn't like to make you.'

How I ever got away with it I still do not understand. Perhaps if I had read and sung I would never have got the part!

After *Follow That Girl*, I at last got a part in a straight play, *Fairy Tale of New York*, without having to do a 'blind' reading. This was simply because I knew Philip Wiseman, the director, and had a chance to see the script before the audition. Because Philip Wiseman was an American, the phrase 'word blindness' was familiar to him; America was much more advanced than Britain in research into reading problems. Wiseman thought it quite natural, because of my 'problem', to let me read several times for him and the author, J. P. Donleavy, while they made up their minds. So it was not the usual 'No-o-o – Next!' and on with the old singing and dancing I had come to expect.

I desperately wanted to act, not sing, and being so young I believed implicitly that I had something to offer, other than just looking the part, that I would be a good actress by the time I was thirty, and that, with the right part, I'd be a star! I had inherited from the Hampshires a positive attitude to work, a driving determination, which was not to leave me for years. Many, with my reading problem, might have thrown in the towel, but somehow the problem itself gave me an extra incentive to survive. I wanted to blot out the memory schoolfriends must have had of me struggling to read Shakespeare, and put a new image in their minds, of someone whom they could like, perhaps even respect and admire.

I had gradually come to realize that doing good work wasn't just up to me: good scripts, good directors, good sets, good costumes, and working with good actors, were also vital. The better the conditions, the easier it is to excel, to break the rules and try something new, to take risks. It was working with Philip Wiseman and J. P. Donleavy that I first experienced this freedom.

J. P. Donleavy, known as Mike, was a soft-spoken man in baggy tweeds, with a 'not quite all there' beard, and a divine wife called Vi. She was from Yorkshire, he was an Irish American, and they lived, with their two children, in a small terraced house in Fulham. I suppose they must have been fairly poor, as at that point Mike had only written *The Ginger Man*, first published in Paris by the Olympia Press, with whom he was having a law-suit which he was fighting himself, since he didn't trust a lawyer to represent him. I believe he owns the Olympia Press now!

Poor or not, Mike and Vi had an ever-open door and there was always something delicious on the stove. We would sit round the table in the first-floor kitchen, while

Philip and Mike discussed *Fairy Tale of New York* and Vi stood at the stove. Mike was uncompromising; he had no desire to 'bend' good work to please other people's mediocre tastes, and Philip agreed with him. No wonder Kenneth Tynan called *Fairy Tale of New York* 'a string of theatrical pearls nourished by a master of comic dialogue'. During the two years I did *Fairy Tale* and the revival of Mike's first play, *The Ginger Man*, at the Royal Court with the brilliant Nicol Williamson, Maggie Tyzack, and T. P. McKenna, the Donleavys, Philip Wiseman and his wife Marie all became close friends. This was a time of teas at Fortnum & Masons, walks in Hyde Park, visits to museums and late night discussions.

We were performing *The Ginger Man* on the night that President John F. Kennedy was shot, and could hear the wailing of people who had just heard the news in the Underground below the Royal Court while we were in our dressing-gowns during the interval. Later in the run, when one of the actors was 'missing', Wiseman went on for him, reading the part from the script – went 'on with the book' in theatrical parlance. I was truly astonished. Acting, moving and *reading* at the same time! Incredible!

I liked Mike and Vi enormously, and when they prospered and moved to the Isle of Man, I longed for my five-day visits there – walking, talking, and eating; it was wonderful to feel that people with good minds accepted me. It was very important to me. I had thought that anyone who could be considered an intellectual would not want to spend two minutes with me. This fear remains with me – I dread meeting bookish people unless I'm on my own ground, discussing a play I am about to do, when I trust that my thoughts are as valid as anyone else's.

In 1961, after *Fairy Tale of New York* and *The Ginger Man* I was lucky enough to play a wonderful lead in a television play, called *Man on a Mountain Top*. An executive from 20th Century Fox saw the play and within days the Fox Company had got me a visa and I was on a plane to America to test for an epic film version of Ernest Hemingway's *Adventures of a Young Man*.

The reason for this sudden move was that at the time most of the major film companies were constantly looking out for the new face to be the new star. I was certainly a new face, and it was sheer luck that my role in the TV play had been such a good one.

The move made my mother misguidedly very happy; it was to make me miserable.

9

WHEN I arrived, too young to be in Los Angeles alone, and by now far too interested in the craft of acting itself to take to Hollywood, I was told I could do the test only if I signed a seven-year contract with Fox. I was called into the casting office and asked what I thought of this wonderful opportunity – to become rich and a star.

'Well, I don't really think I like it,' I said. 'I think I'd be better working in London.' I paused. 'I'm bound to end up just a tart.'

It seemed to me that actresses in Hollywood were either stars, and worked, or ended up as high-class tarts, going out with heads of studios or anyone who could help them towards a movie. I didn't want this.

Sweat broke out on the executive's brow and he squeezed his hairy, beringed fingers together, cracking his knuckles. He coughed.

'But honey you'd be rich.'

He rose and changed the position of the Venetian blinds to keep the sun, that was streaming in, off his neck.

'I'd rather be an actress than be rich.'

'But honey look at Fabian – he's under contract to us – he's got a pool, a Cadillac . . .'

'Who's Fabian?'

When he recovered from the shock of my ignorance, he rose, walked round his desk, and put his arm round me.

'You can't get famous doing art in an attic.' He walked me to the door.

'I want my ticket home,' I said suddenly.

He opened the door and pointed out the accounts department across the lot.

'Collect your weekly expenses,' he said evenly, 'and we'll talk tomorrow.'

I strode out into the heat.

'Honey,' he called after me, 'we're very keen on our girls looking "chic" [pronounced "chik"], we like them to wear high heels, look sexy.'

I looked down at my flat shoes, and cotton milk-maid dress – not a bosom in sight.

'I'll fix for you to go to hairdressing and wardrobe, dear, they'll fix you up.'

He walked back to the telephone and dialled wardrobe and hairdressing.

'I'd still like my ticket home,' I said. 'I'm very homesick and lonely.'

'Lonely?' he said, eyeing me with a new interest. He closed the door and peered down at me. He spoke quietly, as though the office was tapped. 'I can't tonight, honey, but we could go to a pool party Saturday – barbecue. Hedda [Hopper] will be there, Fabian, Ann-Margret, and a new director from France, er . . . you know.'

'No. Who?'

'Can't remember his name, great for Continental movies . . .'

Once out of the office I went off to be 'fixed up'. I'd have been safer in the office.

Two over-groomed, crocodilian ladies, with immaculate red hair, and dressed like Vera Ellen in *Easter Parade*, set about my person.

'Owh, my God, your skin is lovely dear, just take off your clothes, dear, and we'll see what we can do.'

While trying to get out of the wardrobe department before being raped, I was advised always to wear white, to

79

get all my teeth capped and to change the colour of my hair to red.

'You'd look lovely red, dear. Ann-Margret's red, and look what it's done for her.'

The endless costume fittings, hair and wig fittings, executive meetings, script meetings, and contract meetings, dragged on for what seemed like months. I felt trapped and totally impotent. No one would believe I wanted to go home or that I didn't want to sign a seven-year contract – or any contract. Telephone calls across the Atlantic from my agent to the studio seemed to bear no fruit. I was stuck by the pool at the Beverley Crest Hotel with no ticket home. Eventually there seemed nothing for it but to save up my expenses to buy my own ticket home. In the meantime I thought of a foolproof scheme for getting myself freed. I would tell them about my 'word blindness'. I would tell them I couldn't read.

At the next meeting, after I had insulted one of the heads of the studio by telling him that the days of contract artists were numbered, I blurted out, 'And anyway, I can't read.'

'Honey,' he said, 'I love illiterates. They make great actors and great lays.'

Eventually, after nearly six months, my agent turned down the contract, and all the money, and got me out of the country.

I had my next two American offers in 1964 – one from M.G.M. and one from Disney. They were much better deals, tying me down to only one picture a year, for only three years, and for what was then a great deal of money (£17,000, whether I made the pictures or not). I turned them both down. So I never became a film star; but I didn't become a hooker either.

On my return to England, and during my first real spate of unemployment, I sat down to write a book about my experiences in Hollywood. It was called *Pussy on My Shoulder* and it was atrocious, but it helped me to cleanse my mind of Hollywood. I wrote it in longhand, as I have written this book. The difference between then and now is that now I have an invaluable secretary, Jean Ross MacKenzie, who types out each page and automatically corrects the spelling. When I wrote *Pussy on My Shoulder* I was on my own. Here is a sample of the mistakes I made:

Riveiled	Revealed
Convasation	Conversation
Furnature	Furniture
Angelar	Algebra
Had	Hat
Permanatly	Permanently
Maget	Maggot
Unsubsodiyed	Unsubsidised
Where	Were
Were	Where

I had been appalled by my experiences in L.A., and writing this unbelievably bad book did much to get the experience out of my system. On the face of it, it was a curious form of therapy for a dyslexic; yet the daily grind of writing for five or six hours was extraordinarily healing. I enjoyed writing the book, though I was wise enough not to show it to a soul.

By a strange coincidence *Night Must Fall*, in which I had made my dreadful début at Bognor, once again entered my life, and, once again, played an important part in it. I was asked to a screen test for the film version with Albert Finney, this time playing the part of Olivia, the niece and companion, rather than Dora, the maid. The competition was strong, but too pretty for the role – so I got the part.

It was Albert Finney and Karel Reisz, the director, who at last taught me how to approach work professionally, to do 'home-work' before rehearsals, and not just to learn a rough approximation of the lines, but to give real thought to what they meant, and why they were there.

Each morning as I got in the car, and all through the drive to the M.G.M. Studios, I felt sick with fear, so sick that I believed I wouldn't be able to work when I got there. I didn't know *how* to work.

Karel would say, 'Work from strength, from belief in yourself, the belief that what you are doing is right because you know why you are doing it. Make Olivia *strong*.' Strong! I was so overwhelmed by doubts, and so frightened of Karel Reisz and Albert Finney, that I was almost too weak to get off my chair. In Hollywood I had been strong – resolute, fearless – when talking about scripts. But in England it was different. I respected Karel and Albert too much. Hollywood had been a fantasy; this was real.

One day, towards the end of filming *Night Must Fall*, Albert came into my dressing-room. The film version of *Tom Jones* was just about to open in the West End and he was soon to be off to New York to recreate the star part in John Osborne's *Luther*. He walked over to the divan and slumped down on to it. He lay there, clutching his head in his hands, his eyes closed, and asked me if I would hold his head in my hands for a moment. He told me he dreaded the opening of *Tom Jones* and, even more, doing *Luther* in New York. All he wanted was a little reassurance, but I couldn't give it to him.

'Why on earth should you be frightened, Albee,' I asked, 'a great actor like you?'

I wandered up and down, touching things as I passed.

'You know you don't have to worry. You're so good. I don't worry about you. I don't see why you should.'

How little I understood of an actor's needs. I was aware only of my own inadequacies. I have always regretted my lack of understanding at that moment.

As it turned out, his fears about New York proved to be groundless. Broadway was immediately at his feet. *Time* magazine likened his Luther to lightning chained to the floor-boards. *Tom Jones*, of course, turned out to be one of the biggest box office successes of the sixties.

For years I had jogged along, doing the nice little part in the nice little telly play, with no time to rehearse properly, and with the director too busy with the camera script to give the actors any help, and so I had developed some very bad habits. *Night Must Fall* was my chance to get out of the rut, and learn the right way to approach work. Karel and Albert taught me never to turn up to a rehearsal without being properly prepared, having read the script over and over again, thought about the play as a whole, then about my role in relation to the other characters. They taught me the value of research into the period, or the location of a piece, into accents, furniture, clothes, and a thousand and one things that can affect one's general understanding of a play and a character. This does not exclude instinct, gut reaction, or any of the ideas contributed by the director or the other actors: on the contrary, it helps one to work with one's colleagues more effectively.

Now, when I study a script it is a far cry from those non-productive hours, sitting on a lavatory seat, that were such a burden in my childhood. At the very start, I ask for two scripts. The first is the one I keep at home and cover all over with my special 'code'; the second is 'for show'. I keep it in mint condition and take it with me to rehearsals, not wishing my colleagues to know that my real script is a battered document that has hardly been out of my hands since I got it, and is covered in scribbles. I like to give the impression that my work on the script has been effortless, though sometimes, when a second script is unobtainable for some reason, the truth is revealed!

I find that the best way to learn my lines is by repeating the words over and over again *out loud*. If I have to study silently – on a train for instance – I find I cannot absorb the text.

If requires a great effort, but it is worth it because it is part of the job I love.

The average script takes the average actor an hour and a half, or two hours, to read; the same script takes me from three to five hours. In learning lines the ratio is higher. If a colleague takes half an hour to study a scene, I need three hours. I usually work in the middle of the night or very early in the morning, as I hate the threat of the door-bell or the telephone. I like complete quiet, with nothing to break my concentration, even if I only work in half-hour bursts, with frequent stops for a cup of tea, or a pace up and down the room. As the night wears on and it gets colder and colder (I can't put the heating on, not with my upbringing!), I go back to bed with the script, a torch so I can work without waking my husband, a cup of tea, and a hot water bottle.

*　　*　　*

Seeing the rushes at the end of each day's filming of *Night Must Fall* was an experience I would rather have missed. The painful business of watching the work I had done the day before was too often bad for the soul, albeit good for the practical business of getting it better! As a child, when I had taken part in *The Woman in the Hall*, my first film at Pinewood, once, as a treat, they let me go to rushes.

'Let's take little Suzie along after lunch, and see how she likes herself. She's been a good girl and she can see the scene about the sweets.'

This sounded lovely, and I went with my mother and a whole crowd and sat and watched myself, with a thumping heart, in the darkened projection-room.

While the film was still running I slipped from the theatre, found a cupboard, huddled inside, and cried and cried. When everyone wandered back to the stage to start work, I was nowhere to be found. The director sent people running in all directions to locate me and get me back to the set. When eventually they found me, in the dirty cupboard, my face smudged black and still weeping in despair, they tried to get out of me what was the matter.

I sobbed, 'I was awful . . . awful . . . I sound silly . . . squeaky . . . and I look like a baby in that nightie.'

I was given a reassuring cuddle and pushed back to work.

But these things never leave you, and even now when I see rushes I still feel sick and some of the despair of childhood returns. But, of course, I'm too old to hide in a cupboard and cry, much as I'd like to.

Most would-be film producers, directors and writers seem to be on a permanent look-out for a willing pair of eyes to read this or that script, or a book that could be turned into a film. When one begins in the business, one is naturally a keen pair of eyes, the 'would-be' man's dream. My evenings became devoted to reading 'possible film scripts' before daybreak! It got me used to reading scripts, if not to liking it, and trained my powers of judgment. But when I discovered that the 'would-bes' were using me as a guinea-pig, picking my brains and then giving the part – if it materialized – to some other actress, I became less keen. To be fair, the 'would-bes' had no idea that I had to sit up all night reading their masterpieces. I read much more quickly now, and less painfully, but sleep is too precious to waste in chasing a never-to-come-true dream.

*   *   *

I suppose I must have always known that if I applied myself I could learn to read; I never really believed that I could learn to drive a car, still less pass the driving test. The fact that I did pass it, *first time*, is nothing short of a miracle.

Being able to drive has never lost its magic for me. Every time I'm in the car I think to myself, 'Who would have thought I'd be able to do this?'

On my nineteenth birthday I was given a course of twenty driving lessons and went to the British School of Motoring in South Kensington. I did not have a car of my own, and there seemed very little likelihood of getting one. The major problem about driving – the fact that I could hardly tell my left from my right – was worse at that stage of my life since I had not yet admitted to myself that I had a problem. But I was determined to learn. Much of my

85

income was dependent on doing walk-ons and tiny parts in films, and if you could drive in a film, the money was doubled. Driving seemed to be essential.

I have always had a core of seriousness and dedication, and I applied it to my driving lessons. For one thing, I could not possibly afford to fail – I had no money for a second course of lessons and another test.

In order to 'conquer' the mysteries of driving a car I used a method I have since abandoned but found extremely successful at the time. I repeated every instruction my teacher gave me.

'Lights ahead, slow down, brake, clutch, into second, clutch, into first. Stop. Neutral. Hand-brake . . .'

On the day of my test, the examiner must have had the impression that he was examining an examiner.

I knew all the theory backwards – I'd learned it like a parrot – but my inherent disability remained. The result was that I turned left instead of right.

'I said *right*, Miss Hampshire,' the examiner said.

I apologized and said I was nervous. Then I turned right instead of left.

'Left! I said left.'

I pretended I had not heard properly.

At the end of the test, when we finally pulled up in a side street, I was flushed and sticky. I got out of the car, took off my driving shoes and put on my high heels thinking, 'Well at least I didn't kill anybody.'

'Get back in the car, please,' the examiner said.

I settled back in my seat, keyed up and miserable, not knowing what my fate would be.

The examiner sighed and rested his head against the back of his seat, as if the strain of being driven by me had been too much for him.

'Well,' he said, 'you did a nice three-point turn and emergency stop, and your theory was fine. I'm going to give you a pass. But you don't really deserve it.'

I was so overjoyed that I only just heard his final remark.

86

'I'm not sure,' he said, 'that you know your right from your left.'

I got out of the car, brushed the creases from my very plain dress and pushed my Alice band back into place.

The unanimous advice of my friends had been, 'I should tart yourself up a bit, Susan. It's your only hope. No one passes first time.'

Well, by some miracle, I had. I was so glad that I'd ignored the advice and gone looking sensible, and not like some dizzy blonde who doesn't know left from right!

❧ 10 ❧

IN SPITE of all my hard work, pretty well to the exclusion of boy friends, and even ordinary friends, my father felt that I was wasting my time. Worse, he strongly disapproved of my choice of career, feeling that it sullied the family name. When he rang my mother he'd say, 'Why can't the girl go to University – get a degree – do a useful job? She'll have to change her name. I can't have it splashed all over the papers in this dreadful humiliating way.'

He was right. It was dreadful and humiliating – pathetic gossip journalism, about whom I was not going out with or what job I had not got.

'Tell them,' he'd say, 'that she doesn't want to be in the papers. It's very embarrassing for me in the firm. My daughter!'

But at that point I *wanted* to be in the papers, I wanted to be 'famous', and I thought the papers were all part of it. Alas, once you're on the treadmill of rubbish journalism, and have become a name that is easy to ridicule, it is hard to get off. The die is cast. Your image is doomed. You may never be allowed to progress to better things. But that was the Sixties – and in those days I could not even imagine the exhilaration of playing a part like Nora in *A Doll's House*. Ibsen? Never! The classics were way beyond my limited powers. All those words. Impossible!

So the pleas from my father to my mother ('June, someone has just shown me something about Susan, in some ghastly paper. William Hickey? You'd better tell your daughter to do something about it. Get it withdrawn. Haven't you any control over her? Tell her to change her name and for God's sake tell her to get rid of that blonde hair') went unheeded.

He died in 1964, a slow, tragic death, in which every faculty was taken away from him, little by little, until all he could do was smile with his eyes. When I went to hospital to visit him, never often enough, and looked into those eyes, I realized how deeply he loved us all. He had never known how to express it; only now, when he could no longer talk, did the squeeze of his hand and the way he felt the skin of my palm, tell me everything that he had always been too frightened to say to me or to any of his children, perhaps for fear that they did not feel the same love for him. It broke my heart that he had kept that silence, had always wondered, alone, what his children felt for him, never daring to say he cared. If we would just stretch a little, all of us, so much could be cured.

A short time ago, in Scotland, I met several people who had worked with my father.

'Ah,' they said, 'you're so like your father, so hard working, so much his daughter.'

I thought of that brilliant man with his incisive mind. It had never occurred to me that I could be in any way like him – I'd seen so little of him in my life, and had always felt so removed from that powerful brain, and the man who owned it.

*   *   *

For someone who spells so badly it is odd that I should like writing letters so much, but I do. I find writing a note on a postcard easier than telephoning, which involves looking up a number in the directory and then having to remember it long enough to dial it. However I dread receiving letters, except love letters, of course, or letters from the family. A typed letter from a charity, or a solicitor, or an accountant, is a bad beginning to the day. It can wait on the piano for hours to be read. Only when the house is quiet, and I have time to myself, do I knuckle down and decipher it. For years everyone was always saying, 'Do write. We love your letters. They're so funny.' It never crossed my mind that it was my spelling that was 'so funny'; I thought it was my wit!

As a child I wrote to Sir Winston Churchill. I copied the letter out about thirty-five times to get it right. It was at the end of his 'reign' and I wrote disagreeing with a new policy he had adopted – or was it agreeing? However words, even in letters from the great, have never had their true value for me, and I have allowed replies from Sir Winston, Compton Mackenzie, Walt Disney, J. P. Donleavy, to name but a few, all of which would be of great interest to me now, to get lost.

But, like many women, I have kept romantic letters, even though some of them remind me of a time when poor spelling came between me and the one person in the world I wanted to impress. Because of the hours of studying, reading scripts and learning lines, my romantic life had virtually ceased in my teens. My nights were spent poring over scripts. When I met Marcel Marceau in 1964, however, romance took shape again. We met in his dressing-room after a performance of his one-man mime show and, afterwards, I was invited to a party that was being given for him. I remember that he ate almost a whole chicken. His appetite was always amazing.

Our friendship was almost entirely conducted on paper, as Marcel was constantly touring the world. It was during this period of regular letter-writing that my spelling vastly improved, for whenever I even suspected a word was misspelt I took the time to look it up, or rang someone up to check it. It was vital to me that my letters to Marcel should be comprehensible and grammatically correct. My vocabulary, which had been as lamentable as my spelling, took a noticeable leap forward with the help of Roget's *Thesaurus*. The leap was not quite large enough to deceive Marcel into thinking that I was an intellectual, but enough, alas, to make many of my letters appear pretentious! But still, thanks to Marcel, my vocabulary was improving.

I remember once, when he was doing his show in Denmark, I was able to fly out to see it. At the end of the performance he was presented with four hundred carnations which, afterwards, he gave to me.

I had no idea that in the French theatre there is a superstition that carnations are unlucky. I never have carnations in the theatre now or, if I can avoid it, in the house! In fact, the incident so overwhelmed me that it inspired my second venture into literature. I wrote a children's book, called *A Day with the Clown*, about a little girl who was always alone and sad until one day she met a clown. But when he made her happy, she turned into a white cat, so he transformed her back into a sad girl and gave her a flower. Not a carnation.

* * *

The white cat had a special significance for me at the time. As a result of my sudden writing fever I got to know several writers, one of whom said he would teach me five new words a day. The first two words I learned were 'obsequious' and 'sycophant.' The arrangement was working well, and my vocabulary was increasing by approximately twenty-five words a week, when one day I asked my 'teacher' to look after and feed my cat for a week-end. When I got back to my flat after the week-end the cat, a ginger, about nine months old, was nowhere to be seen. The flat was empty, the cat-basket gone, and there was still some milk left in the cat's saucer. I rang my writer friend to find out what on earth had happened. I heard a casual voice at the other end of the line.

'The cat? Oh, I put it in its basket and paid an old lady a fiver to throw it in the river. I felt that the cat was coming between us, and', he added, 'the work'.

Utterly stunned, I dropped the receiver, rushed to the window, and began calling out for my cat. I cried all night, with my head out of the window, howling and howling.

My vocabulary lessons came to an abrupt end and even today I cannot learn a new word without thinking of that poor cat.

*　　*　　*

By 1965 I was earning as much as the Prime Minister; but I knew that the work I was doing was not very good. I was extremely proud of the two Donleavy plays I had done, and I was lucky to have starred in three big films: *The Three Lives of Thomasina* for Walt Disney; *Night Must Fall* with Albert Finney; and *Wonderful Life* with Cliff Richard, but things within me were not right. I was restless. My social conscience had grown out of all proportion and everything I earned I was giving away in some form or another to people I felt needed the money more than I did. I spent on essentials, like a down payment on my cottage; but the place was half empty, containing only the odd chair, a second-hand sofa, a bed, a carpet and a kettle. I paid for singing lessons and voice coaching with Iris Warren, my mentor at the time, but the rest of my money was handed out to others who had debts or troubles. Before I knew what was happening, I was having to take part in really bad films to pay my tax.

In the spring of 1965 I was flying back from New York, having promoted one of the atrocious films I'd made to pay my tax, and was sitting in the plane, dreaming about my proposed trip alone through Russia, taking the Trans-Siberian Railway to Peking. I began to flick through *Life* magazine. I came across a long article on Dr Schweitzer, celebrating his ninetieth birthday. The article spoke of his

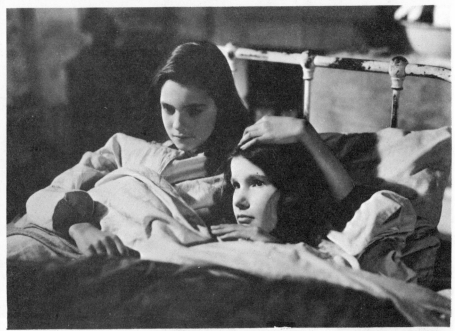

J. Arthur Rank: photograph Max Rosker

My first film role in Woman in the Hall. *This scene shows me with Jill Raymond*

In the title role in The Heartless Princess. *My plain-speaking friend told me, 'Susan, it was lovely, but from the front you look as if you've dipped your nose in a bag of flour.'*

The play that took me to Hollywood: Armchair Theatre's Man on the
Mountain Top. *This photograph shows me with Don Borischenko*

Albert Finney and I in MGM's film version of Night Must Fall in 1963. Albert played Danny, and I took the role of Olivia

Photographs *Jason Shenai*

Three illustrations from my children's book, A Day with the Clown. *When the clown made the sad girl happy, she turned into a white cat*

At Lambarene, in the Gabon, having crossed the River Ogowe to reach Dr Schweitzer's hospital village in 1965

With some of Dr Schweitzer's hospital children

Terence Donovan's portrait of me, taken in about 1962. When Donald Wilson, producer of the Forsyte Saga, *saw the photograph in* Spotlight, *he declared, 'that's my Fleur'. It also secured me my role in* Paris in August

Pierre Granier-Deferre, the director of Paris in August, *who became my husband*

Pierre directing me in Paris in August *in 1965*

With Charles Aznavour in Paris in August

Two scenes from the Forsyte Saga. Above: *Eric Porter as Soames Forsyte and me as his daughter Fleur.* Below: *Martin Jarvis as Jon, with Soames and Fleur*

'reverence for life'. He would not kill even a mosquito, and devoted his own life to running his hospital village in Lambarene in the Gabon, Central Africa. I had a kind of vision of this exceptional man, and it haunted me – I abandoned my plans to go to Peking and decided instead to make a pilgrimage to Lambarene.

There are some investments you make in yourself: my trip to Lambarene was one of these, though in an un-expected way.

I took a plane to Nigeria, then an internal flight into Gabon. A tiny plane took me to the nearest landing-strip to Lambarene, perhaps eight miles away, then I travelled by boat up the river, walked through the jungle and took a canoe to ferry me across the River Ogowe to Lambarene itself.

As I walked up the bank from the river's edge, I saw a man in white, wearing a topee, disappearing behind a small primitive building of wood and corrugated iron. Was this the Doctor? The African who had ferried me across the river pointed out some English and American nurses up the hill and told me, in French, to speak to them if I wished to see The Doctor. I found a nurse called Jean Clent who showed me the way.

'Dr Schweitzer,' I said in French, 'I have come from England to see you.'

I have the impression he answered in English but the moment was so potent that my memory is hazy. Perhaps he spoke in German or even French – whatever the language, I shall never forget what he said.

'As long as you are here, you are my guest.'

I was overjoyed. I had never expected such a generous reception. When I looked at him his eyes twinkled. His soft, droopy moustache covered the smiling corners of his mouth. Never before had I been in the presence of such charm. He looked to the warm-faced nurse, his aide, then back to me, and said something that she translated – I don't know what; I was spellbound. Then he walked on up the hill. I knew that he was someone very special; there was an aura of magic about him.

The events, the feelings, the discoveries of my stay I will always keep to myself – talking or writing about an experience so often devalues it. By the end of my visit I wished only one thing: that I had visited Lambarene twenty-five years earlier, when Schweitzer was at the height of his powers.

Having eaten daily with the Doctor and his staff in the cool dining-room, heard him play the organ, say Grace and exchange interesting conversation, I became spiritually elevated and physically too; each day I was placed further up the table, so that by my last evening, I was in the privileged position of sitting opposite the Doctor. During the meal he told me that the following morning I could spend some time alone with him in his study as he always saw all his visitors privately, if they wished, before they left. I was delighted and agreed.

Throughout my stay, a young man had been following me about, lurking in the shade and watching me as I chatted to the nurses while I helped to roll bandages, asked questions about the python who lived in the trees and had swallowed a whole goat, followed the Doctor on his round, or visited the lepers in their part of the hospital. This boy never spoke to me, he just waited and watched. On my last morning I was rushing to my audience with the Doctor, when I was waylaid by one of the nurses who begged me to spend some time with the young man who had been following me.

'Give him just a few minutes. Cut your time with the Doctor by half. It's important. It'll make such a difference to his life.'

The nurse's plea seemed so urgent that I felt I should change my plans and make my meeting with the Doctor brief. Schweitzer signed his books, *On the edge of a Primeval Forest* and *More from the Primeval Forest*, for me. Then I handed him a copy of Gerald McKnight's *Verdict on Schweit-*

zer. He looked at it and grunted, but though he must have known that it was a highly controversial and uncomplimentary account of his work, he signed it and handed it back to me. I thanked him, we shook hands, he kissed me on both cheeks, gave me a squeeze and we parted.

The nurse hurried me off to see my mysterious admirer. He was half-African, half-Greek, and he was waiting for me at the far end of the village, sitting on a log in the shade. He stood up when he saw me and I seem to remember he wore a blue shirt. I should have remembered everything about him, for it was he, much more than Schweitzer, who was responsible for changing my whole attitude to myself and work. His name was Lombardo.

Lombardo was a misfit. He did not feel part either of African or Greek culture, and he had educated himself through the theatre and the cinema. He had the most amazing knowledge of the new plays that were being performed throughout the world. He knew every director, producer, script-writer, actor. Apart from Lambarene, which had become his haven, the cinema and the theatre were his only solace in life.

He talked and talked, and I listened and thought. When, eventually, I went away I was still thinking.

Earning money for doing a job badly had made me feel deeply ashamed. Yet it was still 'entertainment'. And entertainment, even bad entertainment, had brought extraordinary joy to Lombardo. Was entertainment in itself, then, bad? Perhaps I could do the job I loved, earn a living and improve myself without feeling guilty? Lombardo's strange passion for the arts had made me see clearly for the first time the value of 'entertainment'.

Lombardo promised, when he returned to Greece, to write, and we corresponded for years. He told me what to see, what to read, what plays he thought I should do, and which directors I should work with. I have subsequently had a stab at all the classics that he recommended.

It was extraordinary that in my last half-hour at Lambarene so much of myself that I had gone there to reassess had settled at last, like ground that becomes safe again after a volcano. I understood that we can't all do good work all the time. But whatever work we do we learn from it, and we need not be ashamed of earning a living as we do so.

On the plane home I sat next to a nun who told me that she taught Nigerian children to read. These children could not go to school unless they could find someone to sponsor them for £12-10s a year. It was obviously a cause with which I sympathized and so I decided to sponsor a group of them. For years I received beautifully written thank-you letters and photographs. Then there was an ominous silence. The children, who had been doing so well with their writing, spelling and grammar, had died in the Biafran War.

11

WHILE I was in Africa Ros Chatto had a call from Paris from a production company which needed an English girl, with fluent French, to play opposite Charles Aznavour in a film that was to be shot in Paris in August, called, appropriately *Paris au Mois d'Aôut*. She told them she had several girls who were suitable, and sent off a batch of photographs, one of mine among them. When the director, Pierre Granier-Deferre, saw the photographs, he said the girl he wished to interview was me. Ros, who was aware of my ambivalent feelings towards work at the time, replied that I was in Africa with Dr Schweitzer, that there was some doubt as to when I would return, or whether I would wish to continue to work. But on my arrival home, with my new-found perspective, I was only too happy to fly to Paris. The fact that I spoke only schoolgirl French didn't worry me. I believed that I could learn to speak it adequately in a week; dyslexics have a natural aptitude for languages.

Spelling in French, Spanish and Italian is supposed to be easier for dyslexics than in English, 'for some mysterious reason'. The reason is not mysterious at all. To my mind the English language is so complicated, and cherishes historic idiosyncrasies to such a ridiculous extent, that it is only natural that someone who cannot link the form of a word to its meaning should find French an improvement.

I had my first hurried French refresher course in the ladies cloakroom at Orly Airport, with a woman I had met on the flight, while the producer and director waited and waited for me to emerge from Immigration. When finally I did appear, the producer had given up and was getting his car from the garage to go back to Paris, while the director, Pierre Granier-Deferre, was virtually chewing his cigarette and checking the flight list, furious to have lost most of his Sunday. I was wearing a ludicrously short linen mini-dress and coat, with two huge cotton daisy ear-clips in my ears, and in my hand I was clasping a piece of paper on which I had written the phrases I had learned in my instant French lesson.

'*Je suis desolé d'être en retard, mais j'étais enfermé dans le cabinet,*' I said fluently. M. Granier-Deferre looked bemused but relieved. At least I could speak French.

I kept this bit of paper clutched to me all day. The choice phrases taught to me in the ladies came in very useful and got me the job. Within two weeks or so I was filming in the streets of Paris, shadowed by an amazing, semi-invisible young French teacher, who popped out from behind lamp posts, café doors, and parked cars, to help to teach me the text. She sat with me every evening for hours in the hotel room, helping me with my lines.

The part I was playing was, of all things, that of a chatter-box. The story was about an English model in Paris in August (when all the wives have left their husbands to take the children to the seaside), who has a love-affair with a shop assistant (played by Aznavour) who pretends to be an artist.

Aznavour and Granier-Deferre both knew that a frantic effort to keep up with the French text was going on, but neither of them commented on it at the time.

Aznavour and Granier-Deferre could have been brothers – they both had big, brown eyes and black, arched eye-brows – although Charles was stocky while Pierre was tall and thin. They were both very kind, quiet men. Aznavour would sit on the set with one of his managers, between shots, and play chess. He said he did not count acting as work, more as a rest. Being on stage, alone, for two hours or more, and singing twenty songs – that was work! He had started his stage career as pianist, close companion and driver to Edith Piaf. When she allowed him to sing on stage, he was usually booed off. But now he was one of the world's greatest singing stars and, like Marcel Marceau, applied to himself the most rigid discipline. His private life was also ordered and strong; his children, his wife, were very important and valuable to him.

Pierre Granier-Deferre made me feel that I was the only actress in the world, and his compliments were timed to create good work. He was invariably dressed in grey flannel trousers, Shetland pullovers, and checked shirts. His hands – I always notice hands – were slim, expressive, and wonderful to touch. Towards the end of the film he told me, 'When I saw your photograph and then when I watched your funny walk as you came out of the airport at our first meeting, I said to myself: "I will marry that girl – that is sure." ' By the end of the picture we were passionately in love. 'Passionately' is one of my favourite words, but in this case it exactly describes our feelings.

Marriage had never been uppermost in my thoughts. I had met men I'd wanted to marry but they never seemed to want me – not to marry anyway. In fact, marriage had been so far from my thoughts until I married Pierre that I used to say, when I heard that a friend was getting married, 'Oh no! Poor thing! What a dreadful waste!' But Pierre was different.

So my director became my husband and I learnt *fluent* French at last 'on ze pillow', which is the most comfortable way to learn any language.

When the film was released in Paris in 1965, I had a great deal of personal success, all of which I owed to Pierre. He was, I suppose, the first person ever to say that I was intelligent or a good actress, and both these things were tremendously important to me. Even if he said them simply because he was in love with me, they were a revelation just the same and had a more positive effect on me than almost anything before or since.

For the first time work and love had come together, and existed side by side. In the past, because of my dyslexia, only work had existed because the time that should have been devoted to romance had been used in coping with my disability.

My life had taken a wonderful turn. I had met and fallen in love with a brilliant man who was quiet, artistic and thoughtful. I could now speak fluent French, and was to live and work in Paris; the film was bringing in dozens of offers. Filled with excitement and new-found joy, I rushed back to London to tell the good news to my family. When I arrived, I found that my mother was not at all well.

The shock of my father's death had hit her very badly. For years she had lived in a dream world, imagining that she would spend her old age with him. She had bought a house in Kent that they could share, even though my father had never given any indication that he wanted to go back to her. On the contrary, he had wanted to travel with my brother John, to get to know his son.

As soon as I heard the news of my mother's illness I went to see her doctor, to find out how serious it was. I had a violent shock. He told me that she was riddled with cancer, and had no more than six or nine months to live. He told me that she was not to know she had cancer, and so we had to bear the additional burden of pretending to her that she would get better.

As both my sisters and my brother were married, with young children, and I was the only one who was free, there was no question of going back to France. I had to stay in England, look after my mother, and be with her and the family. It was not a duty or an obligation, it was something I wanted to do. The thought of her dying when she was only sixty-four and still so energetic and full of dazzling magic, seemed inconceivable. The idea of losing her, of her not being in my life, was almost impossible to come to terms with. A blackness enveloped me, and numbed me to the outside world, until well after her death.

When you watch someone die it is hard to believe in death. I sat in my mother's room looking at all the things she had worked so hard for, a pin cushion she had made as a child, a pot, polished a month before. When I thought of her school and all her pupils, whose lives she had enriched, I could not believe that it was all going to vanish. Not a day passed for the following two years when I was not struck at some hour by impossible grief. I was never to know pain like it again, not even when my baby Victoria died. I knew Victoria for only twenty-six hours; I knew my mother for twenty-six years. I carry them both with me.

With the news of my mother's illness I closed up my little room in Paris and accepted a television serial for the B.B.C., which would keep me working in London for the next nine months. Pierre, who had had many years of ill-health himself, understood that while my mother was ill I should be with her, and we agreed to try to get together in Paris whenever we could. I made the excuse to my mother that I didn't want to move back into my little cottage in Fulham as her new mansion flat in Victoria was crying out to be shared, and moved in with her. I started work on *The Forsyte Saga* and watched her slip from us hour by hour.

*   *   *

It is a bitter irony that I would never have played one of the best parts in my career had my mother not been ill and going to die. I think there were three basic reasons why I landed the part of Fleur. The first, curiously enough, was to do with the way in which Galsworthy's novels had been printed. Somewhere in the Sherlock Holmes stories, Doctor Watson observes of a 'three-volume novel' that 'the words were well spaced out, with decent, healthy margins', and this was exactly how the Forsyte novels had been printed.

I could read them very easily and this helped me fall in love with them. When I was interviewed for the part, this love and knowledge showed.

The second reason concerned a photograph. When Donald Wilson, the producer, saw my photo in *Spotlight* he apparently said, 'That's my Fleur.' It was a very remarkable picture, taken by Terence Donovan,* but even so Donald Wilson's intuition was extremely brave: up to then I had not played any part that suggested I would be right for the complex and difficult character of Fleur.

The third reason sounds absurd, but I firmly believe that it contributed. When the producer arrived at the restaurant where he had arranged to interview me, he found me speaking French to the waiters and Fleur was supposed to be half French!

*   *   *

The Forsyte Saga changed my working life, and being with my mother while working on it gave me a tremendous insight into the period. She spoke to me so often of the Twenties; how girls had suddenly started thinking and walking differently, their movements changing because the new clothes were so free, unrestrictive and liberating – body language is very important in a visual medium.

The script of *The Forsyte Saga* was extremely faithful to John Galsworthy's books, and I knew the books backwards, as I had read them many times since having been asked to play Fleur Forsyte. The result was that for the first time, the regular read-throughs every ten days of each new episode were *not* a nightmare. Fleur's sentences were short and, as is usually the case with a television script, well spaced, and clearly laid out on the page, like this:

---

* The same photograph had got me the interview and ultimately the film with Pierre. Pierre often said that he was in love with that photograph.

MIX:

2. INT.HALL. SOUTH SQUARE. DAY

(FLEUR LETS HERSELF IN AT THE FRONT DOOR
AND IS ABOUT TO GO STRAIGHT UPSTAIRS WHEN
SOAMES COMES OUT OF THE DRAWING ROOM.)

SOAMES: There you are ... still rattling
about.

FLEUR: Not any more Duckie. The canteen's
finished. I'm out of a job.

SOAMES: Good thing too. Wearing yourself
to a shadow. I should think you'd be glad
to have more time for Kit. He's a rascal.
What d'you think he asked me for this morning?
A hammer!

FLEUR: He loves breaking things up.

SOAMES: H'm .. children. We weren't made
such a fuss of when I was young.

FLEUR: You make more fuss of him than anyone.
Did you give him one?

SOAMES: Hadn't got one. What should I be
doing with a hammer? Well ... the little
chap's got a twinkle.

FLEUR: Mercifully. Did you spoil me?

SOAMES: Can't tell. Do you feel spoiled?

FLEUR: When I want things, I want them.
(SOAMES STARES AT HER, THEN TURNS AWAY.)

SOAMES: Yes ... I dare say but you're not
unique in that.

I can read the above type of script with reasonable fluency, whereas at first sight the average play baffles me, as in the example taken from G. B. Shaw's *Man and Superman* on pages 106 and 107

* * *

I cannot read these pages at sight, I need hours and hours of preparation. Also shown is an example of my code for this particular piece.

It is rare for a project to be both good and popular, but *The Forsyte Saga* was both, thanks to brilliant casting and Galsworthy's highly televisable books. (Often a less than great book makes first-class television, whereas a first-class book does not necessarily make great television, television being a second-rate medium in itself.) For a project to be good, popular, and happy to work on, is even rarer, so the 'Saga' was a unique experience for everyone involved. Donald Wilson, the producer and writer of most of the episodes, whose brain-child it was, David Giles, the director of three-quarters of the episodes, and James Cellan-Jones, the director of my first seven episodes, headed an enchantingly happy team, which, considering that there were two hundred speaking parts, can have been no easy task. One reason for this harmony was that the twenty or so major parts were so good. Actors are not restless if they are 'in love' with their roles, and most of us were. Each character was so rich and three-dimensional and there was the added joy of developing it little by little with each episode. The scope for depth of interpretation was amazing.

Eric Porter's Soames was a masterpiece and he was a joy to work with. When we started a scene, he would say, 'I think perhaps, Susan, we should do it like this . . .' and I would thrust my hands over my ears and insist, 'Don't tell me, don't, I don't want to know. Let me do it.' We worked together in harmony with great understanding. He had beautiful, fine hands and perfect nails, and he always rehearsed in a sailing cap. His eyes and eyebrows reminded me of Pierre. He was never moody or difficult, as one might have expected, given the size of his role and the responsibility he bore. Nicholas Pennell, who played Michael Mont so well, and the wonderful Maggie Tyzack who was a splendid Aunt Winifred, were equally endearing.

Most weekends I would go off to Paris to see Pierre, having taken care of my mother all week, and Eric would say to David Giles, 'You can't let her go off like this. It's too great a risk. Supposing the plane crashes – who's going to play my daughter? They'd have to re-write all the last episodes.' Then he'd walk off and sit on his own and roll a cigarette with those beautiful hands.

However, I still went to Paris every weekend. It didn't trouble me – it was like hopping on a bus.

I was still highly self-conscious about my reading and wondered if my colleagues noticed anything odd. I have since asked some of them. Kenneth More said, 'I have no recollection whatsoever of your having reading difficulties. Dyslexic? No.'

When I asked David Giles, he said, 'At the read-throughs I used to think "Oh dear, Susan doesn't like the script – she's frowning when she reads it."' James Cellan-Jones had heard something about my problem and was surprised that I was always word perfect. Maggie Tyzack said,

I had no idea you were dyslexic when we worked together. Along with many other people, I'm afraid I didn't know the condition existed. I seem to remember thinking that you always took read-throughs very seriously. If I thought about it at all I probably assumed you were short-sighted. I only learned of your handicap when you let it be known through your work for fellow dyslexics. I think the distress caused by the disability must be made far worse by the ignorance of one's fellows, rather like the lack of understanding of migraine which has nothing in common with a headache other didnt choose to be cut to your measure. And I wont be cut to it.

ANN: Nobody wants you to, Jack. I assure you – really on my word – I dont mind your queer opinions one little bit. You know we have all been brought up to have advanced opinions. Why do you persist in thinking me so narrow minded?

TANNER: Thats the danger of it. I know you dont mind, because youve found out that it doesnt matter. The boa constrictor doesnt mind the opinions of a stag one little bit when once she has got her coils round it.

ANN [*rising in sudden enlightenment*]: O-o-o-o-oh! now I understand why you warned Tavy that I am a boa constrictor. Granny told me. [*She laughs and throws her boa round his neck.*] Doesnt it feel nice and soft, Jack?

TANNER [*in the toils*]: You scandalous woman, will you throw away even your hypocrisy?

ANN: I am never hypocritical with you, Jack. Are you angry? [*She withdraws the boa and throws it on a chair.*] Perhaps I shouldnt have done that.

TANNER [*contemptuously*]: Pooh, prudery! Why should you not, if it amuses you?

ANN [*shyly*]: Well, because – because I suppose what you really meant by the boa constrictor was this [*she puts her arms round his neck*].

TANNER [*staring at her*]: Magnificent audacity! [*She laughs and pats his cheeks.*] Now just to think that if I mentioned this episode not a soul would believe me except the people who would cut me for telling, whilst if you accused me of it nobody would believe my denial!

ANN [*taking her arms away with perfect dignity*]: You are incorrigible, Jack. But you should not jest about our affection for one another. Nobody could possibly misunderstand it. You do not misunderstand it, I hope.

TANNER: My blood interprets for me, Ann. Poor Ricky Ticky Tavy!

ANN [*looking quickly at him as if this were a new light*]: Surely you are not so absurd as to be jealous of Tavy.

I underline all the words of my part

words that are unusual and that I need to watch out for

assure   words that I need to stress to get the sense

P.P.   softly

boa constrictor

~~didnt choose to be cut to your measure. And I wont be cut to it.~~

ANN: Nobody wants you to, Jack. I assure you – really on my word – I dont mind your queer opinions one little bit. You know we have all been brought up to have advanced opinions. Why do you persist in thinking me so narrow minded?

TANNER: Thats the danger of it. I know you dont mind, because youve found out that it doesnt matter. The boa constrictor doesnt mind the opinions of a stag one little bit when once she has got her coils round it.

ANN [*rising in sudden enlightenment*]: O-o-o-o-oh! now I understand why you warned Tavy that I am a boa constrictor. Granny told me. [*She laughs and throws her boa round his neck.*] Doesnt it feel nice and soft, Jack?

TANNER [*in the toils*]: You scandalous woman, will you throw away even your hypocrisy?

ANN: I am never hypocritical with you, Jack. Are you angry? [*She withdraws the boa and throws it on a chair.*] Perhaps I shouldnt have done that.

TANNER [*contemptuously*]: Pooh, prudery! Why should you not, if it amuses you?

ANN [*shyly*]: Well, because – because I suppose what you really meant by the boa constrictor was this [*she puts her arms round his neck*].

TANNER [*staring at her*]: Magnificent audacity! [*She laughs and pats his cheeks.*] Now just to think that if I mentioned this episode not a soul would believe me except the people who would cut me for telling, whilst if you accused me of it nobody would believe my denial!

ANN [*taking her arms away with perfect dignity*]: You are incorrigible, Jack. But you should not jest about our affection for one another. Nobody could possibly misunderstand it. You do not misunderstand it, I hope.

TANNER: My blood interprets for me, Ann. Poor Ricky Ticky Tavy!

ANN [*looking quickly at him as if this were a new light*]: Surely you are not so absurd as to be jealous of Tavy.

😟 Granny

⌒· pause

/ / breaks between words to help me see them more clearly

✗ attack

than the location of the pain. Actually, Sue, your much battered and dog-eared script gave me a bit of an inferiority complex; as Angela Brazil's heroines would say, I felt you were a 'bit of a swot'.

Towards the end of the 'Saga' I began to realize that I had done something which was really important to me. Apart from offers pouring in, I was deluged with letters, but these were not the usual sort of fan letters. They were from actors, writers, directors, people who had been actresses in the 1920s, and old movie stars. People would come up to me in the street and say, 'Oh, you wicked little thing, you wicked little thing.' The public got very involved.

In John Fisher's *The World of the Forsytes** I was quoted as saying:

I didn't feel a bit like Fleur, and so didn't identify myself with her. But I loved her dearly with every fault that she had, and some of them were enormous. I mean, I really cared about her, which was surprising because one would not have expected that the actual person who was playing an unsympathetic character would have liked her so much. But she was very true to life and this was *why* she was attractive to so many people; all her faults were such human ones . . .

Like her father, she felt the need for the affair of a lifetime – the 'grand amour', and was ready to cross the world to get it, just as if she were blindly following a star.

I felt also that she was suffocated by her money, her father, her weak husband. She had everything against her and she was fighting to get out, and therefore she would fall into little mediocre interests in order to have some outlet. She was before her time; forty years later she would

* From *The World of the Forsytes* by John Fisher, published by Secker & Warburg in 1976.

have married later in life and she wouldn't have done a stupid old-fashioned thing like marrying on the rebound. She stood for all that was feminine and her restlessness was probably typical of the Twenties.

My mother's illness had changed the course of my life. I had given up what I thought might be a good career in France, yet the part I had taken to stay close to her was certainly my best to date. My mother and I were exchanging 'favours'. That I was to lose her, and that she would not be there to see Pierre and me married, or know the extent of the success of the 'Saga', was a sadness I took years to overcome.

She died at four one morning. I thought I could keep her alive a little longer with freshly squeezed orange juice, but the doctor said she was already dead, although her heart went on beating until eventually there was a sigh, and it stopped. We were all with her; all heart-broken.

My mother had started her school for me; had she not done so, I would have been tormented like other dyslexics. But she had formed a protective world round me to reduce my suffering to the minimum, and to help me to learn, anticipating, by many years, the type of remedial help available today.

In the months that followed I wrote letters to her and took them to her grave. I have never been able to understand why I chose this way of trying to communicate with her – laboriously writing letters and then digging them into the earth. Perhaps I was trying to show her that I could write, could spell, that I had accepted the disability which, without her amazing care and love, might have crippled me.

12

PIERRE AND I were married in May 1967, towards the end of making *The Forsyte Saga,* and when the serial was screened my head was in the clouds. It created a tremendous buzz around the country and I was thrilled to be part of it. So when I was asked to read a children's story on *Jackanory* by the B.B.C. I was flattered, and not as wary as I should have been. I did explain that I would not be able to read the story from the teleprompter, like the other actresses, but would have to learn the whole book, but the producer said, 'Don't worry, Susan. It'll be easy. Do say yes. You'll love it. We've found a perfect story for you – about hamsters! It'll only take a day.'

I agreed and settled down to learning a whole children's book in a few days. It was impossible. I just could not do it. I was exhausted after nine months' work on the 'Saga', my mother's death and all the business of getting married. I hadn't had a break and the words simply wouldn't go into my brain. I sat up night after night, and the pressure of knowing that I had only four days in which to learn the book added to the difficulty. Eventually, the day for taping the show loomed up and I felt so impotent that it was like being back at school. I had already asked my agent to ring the B.B.C. to see if there was any way in which I could postpone the job, but the reply had simply been, 'Tell her not to worry. There's a teleprompter. She can use that. Everyone else does.'

It seemed that the fact that I could not read from a teleprompter was impossible for the B.B.C. to comprehend.

On the day of the recording I left my house feeling very nervous and unsure, and arrived at the studio pinched, fraught and physically sick. The thought of having to read aloud, not only in front of the whole studio and camera crew, but in front of several million people, numbed me. Pierre, who delivered me to the studio, held my hand, kissed me, then slipped away, leaving me to the tender mercy of the floor-manager, who jollied me along to make-up. My legs would hardly move and the corridor seemed endlessly long.

Once inside the studio, the feeling of emptiness in my head that I had had as a child returned. I looked at the book and couldn't see it. The more I panicked the less I could see. I couldn't even see where I was, and when invited to sit on the chair, I missed it, and nearly fell on the floor. I talked very fast, getting everyone's name wrong, saying silly things and laughing a lot. When I'm nervous I invariably behave like the dumb blonde that most people seem to assume I am. But inside I'm thinking, why am I pretending to be a fool? I've more sense in me than half these people, yet I'm behaving like a nut-case, indelibly printing on their minds the idea that I'm a useless fool.

By the time I was sitting in front of the camera with the book on my lap, ready for me to read, I thought that my head had finally turned into a ball of string, and that I had gone blind. Everything was out of focus – the book, the teleprompter, all was a blur. People spoke, I replied 'yes' and laughed, but I could not hear what they had said. All coordination had gone.

It is well known that dyslexics are at their worst under pressure and I was no exception. Sweat poured from me, my breathing became erratic and my head felt like a block of wood.

Why hadn't I been strong and said beforehand, 'this is a

job I *cannot* do. *I cannot read*'? The truth was that I still could not admit it. It was still half a secret.

I was now not only sweating, blind, uncoordinated and laughing inanely, but starting to shake as well. Have they noticed, I thought? Do they know what is going on inside me?

The sweet, patient producer came up to me every time I faltered, and in soothing tones said, 'Don't worry, Susan, there's plenty of time.' But I knew there was not plenty of time. In fact we were running out of time fast.

As the end of the day drew near a compromise of some kind seemed inevitable. It was decided that I should memorize small sections of the script, to be used as a voice-over, with illustrations from the story. But from time to time the camera had to focus on my face, and the memory of it makes me sweat all over again. My blank expression and dead eyes were a tragic sight, and all because I was not able to do the most normal thing in the world – read.

At the end of each sentence I would stop as though frozen and try to grasp the words in the book or on the teleprompter. I could no longer recognize the symbols even of my own 'code', a system of colours, signs and lines that I have built up over the years to help me to recognize the meaning of a sentence or to pick out a word. In the pit of my stomach lay the pain of frustration and humiliation. But by the end of the day I could not feel anything at all. I was paralysed. All I wanted was to get out of the studio and home to Pierre.

When the programmes were screened a friend who saw them said, 'It was very strange, Susan, they kept stopping you in the middle of the story. Is that normal? It looked as though you'd forgotten your lines, but I know you never do that.'

I don't imagine that the B.B.C. have used a dyslexic on *Jackanory* again. When I remember incidents like *Jackanory* it amazes me that I ever managed to discover reading for pleasure. But I did.

In 1974, after doing *Vanity Fair* and *The First Churchills* for the B.B.C., I became pregnant, and decided to give up work for the time being. At the age of thirty a new dimension came into my life – leisure! And three new experiences: expecting, relaxing, and reading for pleasure rather than as part of my work.

Dostoevsky's *Crime and Punishment* was the first book I tackled. It possessed me completely and I wept when I arrived at the final page and had to close the book for the last time. After *Crime and Punishment*, and Tolstoy's *War and Peace*, Pierre just handed me the books he felt I would enjoy. I read copiously during those months, including books on natural childbirth and Joy Adamson's *Born Free* and *Living Free* about Elsa the lioness, since I was scheduled to play Joy Adamson in the next Elsa film, *Living Free*, five months after the baby was born.

With the help of natural childbirth, I fearlessly and painlessly produced (a month early!) a son. I was staying in the house that was my mother's in Sandwich, and so Christopher was born in the hospital at Canterbury. Pierre held my hand and I cracked very bad jokes, so he wouldn't be frightened.

§ 13 §

As I have already shown, like many dyslexics I have never really been able to tell left from right; and this deficiency has caused me a great deal of embarrassment, most of which I prefer to forget. However, one embarrassing occasion I should record concerns my sister Ann.

Ann was a wonderful pianist and once, at the end of months of intensive work on some Mozart Sonatas, she recorded them on a friend's tape-recorder as a means of charting her progress. The tape lay on the top of her piano, among hundreds of sheets of music, for ages. Being totally without vanity, she never listened to it, so when I wanted to work on a Swedish accent for a film, I asked her to lend me the tape and let me use the other side. I promised not to wipe off her recording, and to return the tape in a day or so. She lent it willingly and I recorded a Swedish friend's voice to which I then listened over and over again. I had carefully marked the tape so I would not wipe Ann's side, but instead of running it from left to right, I ran it from right to left and erased her recording. Ann never complained, but it was an act of carelessness on my part for which I can never forgive myself.

I should, in passing, make it clear that a tape-recorder is not a vital piece of equipment for me. 'Do you learn your lines with a tape-recorder?' is a question I, and even actors who are not dyslexic, get asked over and over again. I learn my lines by reading them and re-reading them very slowly. I learn what they *mean*. Very few actors learn their lines, parrot fashion, from tape-recorders. For one thing, the voice pattern on the tape sinks into the subconscious and reproduces itself in a scene, leaving no room for development, interpretation, imagination and truthful response.

Another incident I recall, when my inability to distinguish left from right got me into a mess, happened during that first disastrous trip to Hollywood. I had hired a white Thunderbird convertible, and as I drove down Wilshire Boulevard with the top down and my hair streaming in the wind, I felt I must be the most attractive girl in town. Everyone, but everyone, was turning his head to look at me. 'This is great,' I thought, 'Los Angeles has done something for me after all.' When I got to the lights I pulled up to find myself face to face with an oncoming car. I was on the wrong side of the road! I had kept reminding myself to keep to the right and had duly kept to the left! Alas, it explained all those turned heads. Nobody had been admiring my blond hair; they'd been waiting for the inevitable head-on smash.

When Pierre, Christopher and I moved out to Kenya to do *Living Free*, knowing left from right turned out to be essential. Christopher was five months by now, and I was on the last lap of breast-feeding him. Brenda, the nanny, was giving him bottle feeds when I was at work.

I had lost nearly a stone, but I was still more than a stone overweight, and after the first costume-fitting in Nairobi I was told I had to lose at least fifteen pounds by a given date – or out! I lost the weight not, as one might expect, through terror at the thought of working with lions, but by a diet of pineapple, fried eggs, tomatoes and lettuce!

The first time I met the lions I shook all over. I've never known fear like it, every muscle in my body trembled. Then the day came when Nigel Davenport, my co-star, and I were summoned to a photo-call near Lake Nivasha. We arrived, after a very dusty drive, decked out in safari gear that was already sticking to our bodies. No sooner were we out of the jeep than we heard a voice calling across the compound, 'Now, Susan and Nigel, as we've got the introductions with the big cats over, we'll do a little photo-call with the smaller cubs.'

Smaller cubs! They looked like huge great lions to me. Nigel and I gave no visible signs of panic except for laughing and joking a lot as we took our positions.

'Susan, stand with the two smaller cubs on your right.'

Instant panic. My right, God help me, which is my right? I began walking – in the wrong direction, naturally. These were the positions we were supposed to take up:

NIGEL ME CUB CUB ELSA

And these were the positions we ended up in:

NIGEL CUB CUB ELSA ME

The cub I was supposed to be standing by had been tethered, so that I should be completely safe; instead I found myself standing next to a three-hundred-pound lioness.

As I looked down at Elsa, only a foot away from my feet, I felt faint. I wondered if I should scream, or run back to the jeep, but I had been warned that any sudden movement or sound is disastrous when working with the big cats. I stood still and said steadily, 'Please, could someone help to move me – or Elsa.' My voice was quiet and polite.

The trainer, Hubert Wells, laughed as he strolled over. (He only used a rope and leather gloves to keep the animals under control. He never carried a gun or used any drugs.)

'Don't worry, Susan,' he said, jovially, 'the cub you're *supposed* to be next to is tethered. Why don't you slowly take two steps back – but keep looking at Elsa – then walk quietly to the other side where you're meant to be. The cats are all relaxed. There's no need to worry. I'm here. Just move slowly.' I did – nothing happened – and my confidence and trust in Hubert Wells began to grow.

After that first day, I made rapid progress with the big cats and was able to work with them fearlessly; so much so that Jack Couffer, the director, and Hubert Wells always put me between Nigel Davenport and Elsa. Elsa could smell that I wasn't frightened, while Nigel, as he readily admitted, was 'shit scared', and Elsa could scent it. This was one of the rules I had to learn about lions – conquer your fear, otherwise they smell it, and play up. There were other rules for survival: never turn your back on big cats; always walk away from them backwards – as with Royalty!; never crawl or lie down in their presence, they will think you are prey; never move quickly or make sharp movements. Also, it is better if you don't drink or smoke or do anything that will dull your wits while working with them. None of the professional trainers touched a drop. These were not old circus animals, worn out after years of performing tricks; they were young, beautiful and powerful. One flick of a tail could knock you for six, one bite from their perfect teeth into your jugular vein could kill you in sixty seconds.

Towards the end of the filming, when the trainers thought I could cope with anything as far as the lions were concerned, I was asked to run through the bush, between trees, chasing Elsa as though we were frolicking together. I thought it would be impossible, but Hubert Wells proved it wasn't. Elsa was fed, kept in the shade and rested, and in the afternoon, when the sun was no longer so powerful, she was let loose – and I with her.

I found myself chasing a semi-wild lioness around the bush, with the camera crew a hundred yards or more away, too far away to come to my rescue if things took a nasty turn. But Herbert had already thought of that and had worked out a device to prevent it. If Elsa had my hat in her mouth she would be unlikely to go for me; she'd want me to chase her and try to retrieve the hat. I believed him. Rehearsals were out – Elsa would have become stale and my courage might have waned.

I heard 'Action', and suddenly I was chasing Elsa through the long grass.

'Susan, keep running, she's coming round on your right. Run to your right.'

My right – of course. I veered to the left, and ran straight into the lioness.

'Keep going, Susan, run faster. Hedge her in on the left. Bring her into shot. On the LEFT, Susan, LEFT.'

Left, right, right, left – how could I tell the difference? I was too busy trying to keep up with Elsa, trying to overcome my fear, trying to appear carefree and sporty. Elsa was tiring of the game. She was playfully butting me with the hat, then moving off. How could I hedge her in, if I kept moving to the right when it should have been left? If I didn't hedge her in quickly enough she might escape into the bush and it might take days to find her. It was my responsibility to respond quickly to the shouts of 'left' and 'right', to keep Elsa in shot, and make it appear as though we romped about like this every day.

'Cut. Cut.'

I've never been so glad to hear that word, or to be told that the 'take' had been a good one. The film was important from the conservation point of view, and I very much wanted to achieve the naturalness and ease that Joy Adamson herself displayed with Elsa. After that little romp I wrote a great 'R' on my right palm and an 'L' on my left, and kept them there till the end of the shooting. In fact, I never needed these visual aids; my final scenes with Elsa were static, though even more alarming. I had to lie down with her on a camp bed and appear to go to sleep.

They gave Elsa a good feed and put the camp bed in the shade under a huge thorn-tree. When Elsa was nicely settled, I was asked to lie down beside her, top to tail, with nothing on but a pink swimsuit. There was hardly room for both of us on the narrow bed. Elsa's tail swished and flicked across my body landing on my bare skin like a thick whip. I tried to master my fear – and I succeeded. I felt a tremendous sense of pride and achievement. It was only when we were all packed up and getting on the plane to come home that I felt truly frightened. I kept shaking and thinking 'I could be dead – I could be dead.'

❧ 14 ❧

WHEN WE got back from Africa in the summer of 1971, I took Christopher to see his paediatrician, Dr White Franklyn, for a routine check-up. Among the usual list of questions was this: were there any hereditary diseases in my family?

'None, so far as I know,' I replied, then added, 'Except that I can't read very well.'

'Dyslexic?' the doctor asked casually. For a moment I did not reply. *Dyslexic.* I suppose I'd heard the word before but it did not mean anything to me. Eventually I said something idiotic, like, 'Er, dyslexic?'

Dr Franklyn looked at me shrewdly.

Then, very kindly, he explained that he was on the Kershaw Committee, a body organized by the Council for the Rehabilitation of the Disabled, and he asked me if I would be prepared to be 'screened' by Dr Jan Kershaw, the chairman, and his colleagues later in the year. I agreed.

A few months later I found myself standing before Dr Kershaw, Dr A. White Franklin, Professor A. Tropp, Mr G. W. S. Gray, Mr Colin Stevenson, Professor G. P. Meredith and Professor T. R. Miles, feeling like a performing squirrel as I attempted to 'sequence' numbers, read aloud, spell 'scissors' and 'decision', do my tables, write with my left hand, then my right, and generally make a fool of myself as I had at school.* At the end of this sweat-producing ordeal, the Committee gave their verdict. There was no doubt. I was dyslexic.

So there it was. My disability had a name at last and, above all, it was a *legitimate* disability. It was a curious revelation to receive at the age of thirty.

You would have thought that, after twenty-five years of trauma, I would have shouted the news from the roof tops.

'It's all right. We know what it is. It's dyslexia!'

But no. I kept it a secret – from my family, my agent, from everyone except Pierre – and to him I mentioned it only in passing.

'They've discovered I have all this trouble because I'm dyslexic – what do you want for supper?'

*   *   *

After Christopher was born, I seemed to be almost per-manently pregnant. Every time I went abroad to start a new film, no sooner had I got off the plane than I seemed to find myself ringing Pierre in Paris to say, 'I'm pregnant again.' Christopher would get very excited at the prospect of a little brother or sister, and Pierre was always kind. But the pregnancies never lasted long. Usually, at the third or fourth month, I'd be zoomed off to hospital and then driven home in a mini-cab, grey-faced and silent after yet another miscarriage. On one occasion I nearly died.

But with Victoria it was different. I took tremendous care during the first few months, quietly following Pierre around wherever he was filming. Christopher and I joined him in Corsica, where he was directing a film with Yves Montand, and we walked, played on the beach, rested, and I felt sick all the time.

The delight of being an Englishwoman married to a Frenchman was that I was exempt from all intellectual

* A copy of one of their test forms is reproduced on pages 156-9.

inquisitions. Although, like many reasonably cultivated French, we moved in fairly literary circles, the language barrier – despite the fact my French was fluent – excused all. I could sit and listen, but never be *expected* to contribute.

When I was over four months pregnant I was asked to do Ibsen's *A Doll's House* at the Greenwich Theatre for three weeks, and, as I was feeling so well, I couldn't resist. Apart from the enormous size of the part and the tarantella in the second act, there was no risk to my health and I felt more than up to it. The baby didn't show, and as I'd got safely to four and a half months, I felt it would be safe to tackle Nora and then rest for the next months. Most people work up to the sixth or eighth month. When asked who I would like to direct, I said Ingmar Bergman and promptly wrote to him.

A telegram I have treasured came in reply:

GN TLX 886891 ZCZC SLB380 STOCKHOLM 33 18 1039
NORTHERN EL ELT SUSAN HAMPSHIRE LONDON SW10
DEAREST SUSAN I THINK YOU WILL BE THE MOST
WONDERFUL NORA IN THE WORLD UNFORTUNATELY
MY SCHEDULE IS PLANNED UNTIL SPRING 1974
WITH ALL GOOD WISHES   INGMAR

Though part of me wanted to admit to the world that I was dyslexic, I could not do it. I thought that if I did, it would affect my chances of getting work, and I remained extremely cagey. At the first reading of *A Doll's House*, with Sylvia Syms, who had already played Nora and was now playing Mrs Linde, I did my usual trick of three-quarters learning the part, pretending to read it, and, just before the reading, announcing, 'I suppose you all know I read very badly,' then plunging into the text.

At the end of reading the first act, I was so exhausted with the effort of half-reading that the director, Michael Wearing, said we would 'plot' the first act after lunch and not read the second act. Relief.

A Doll's House played to standing room only, and was on the whole critically very successful. It was very exciting for me. Sometimes reviews can teach: Michael Billington of *The Guardian* suggested that I should in some way give more emphasis to the dilemma of a young woman leaving her two children for spiritual freedom and development. Ibsen provides no specific words to suggest this, but Billington had made a valuable point. One does not need words – a body movement, a look, a pause, a gesture can do it, and from then on I tried to give the part this extra element.

I was still enjoying the success of *A Doll's House* when out of the blue I got an enormous tax demand – to be paid immediately, as always. I had just taken four months off, and was now working for £30 a week. I had a child, a nanny, a busy life, and all the expense of constantly travelling between London and Paris. In the previous year I had done almost no work, because of Christopher. I had no reserves in the bank and my current living expenses were high.

Ros Chatto rang to ask if I felt up to doing a filmed musical version of *Dr Jekyll and Mr Hyde* with Kirk Douglas – a little singing, a little dancing, and riding a bicycle. I was six months pregnant, but the tax had to be paid *somehow* and the money from the film would exactly cover the demand. It was a grim prospect but as soon as my three weeks at Greenwich were over I started on the film.

In the scene where Kirk Douglas and I had to kiss, the baby kept kicking Mr Douglas, who said to my close friend and stand-in, Joy Adams, 'This is the only time I've kissed a leading lady and been kicked below the belt at the same time.'

The film was rapidly running out of money and the actors were complaining they were not getting paid. As I was only doing the film to pay my tax I HAD to get paid, so each Monday I would refuse to go on the set until I had my cheque in *my hand*. I would then give it to the driver to deliver to my agent so she could have it cleared immediately. Only then would I consent to work.

'You can't let a pregnant woman work without being paid – the cheques are my craving, like chocolate fudge,' I'd say.

It was lucky for me that I had these 'cravings', and that I was bold enough to insist on a cheque in my hand, as I was one of the few artists on the film to be paid.

By the end of the filming I was not feeling too good, but to my great relief the tax was paid, and I could take Christopher to my in-laws in Switzerland, rest and enjoy the last months of pregnancy. We'd been in Villars for less than a week when the baby suddenly decided to arrive – at seven months. My sister-in-law drove with me in the ambulance to the Lausanne Hospital, where some hours later the baby was born. Half asleep I rang Pierre. He was in Paris and it was the middle of the night.

'Pierre, you've got a little girl – 2lbs 6 ozs. What shall we call her?'

'Victoria,' he said sleepily.

'She's not very well – she's so small.'

'I'll come immediately.'

Within a few hours he was there, standing in the room, looking out of the window. He had been asked by the doctors to tell me that Victoria had died.

I had never held her. I did not even know if she had been christened.

'I knew she'd die,' I said. 'You'd better tell everyone – but I don't want any one to send letters or flowers. Nothing. I'll just sleep. But I'd love a biscuit to have with my tea – if you could get some.'

He scoured Lausanne for English biscuits and came back to my room.

'I'm sorry about Victoria,' he said, 'but she was small – and maybe it's best.'

'Maybe,' I said, but I did not mean it. In my heart I was cursing the Inland Revenue because they had taken my child.

A visit to Sweden for the re-run of The Forsyte Saga. *To my left is Ingmar Bergman, and to my right Nicholas Pennell, who played Fleur's husband Michael Mont in the* Saga

Me as Becky Sharp in the BBC serial of William Thackeray's Vanity Fair *in 1967*

Photograph BBC

Two scenes from The First Churchills. Above: *John Neville as John Churchill with me as Sarah Jennings, before their marriage. Below:* me as Sarah Churchill, then Lady Marlborough, with John Standing as Sidney Godolphin and Margaret Tyzack as Princess Anne

BBC's serial of Anthony Trollope's Palliser novels in 1974. This photograph shows me as Glencora, Duchess of Omnium, shortly before her death, with Philip Latham as my husband, Plantaganet

With one of the lion cubs while filming Living Free *in 1971*

Two photographs taken on location in Kenya while shooting the film. Above: Nigel Davenport and I following at a respectful distance behind the lioness who played Elsa. Left: *a close encounter with Elsa*

Joy Adamson with me and my son Christopher during the shooting of Living Free

East African Standard

With Christopher

Playing Nora in A Doll's House *at the Greenwich Theatre*

Me as Ann Whitefield with Richard Pascoe as Jack Tanner in the RSC's production of Man and Superman *in 1977*

My wedding day, 4 April 1981, with Eddie at Chelsea

Photograph Richard Young Features

My attempt to embroider 'passionately loved' on a handkerchief

Photograph Jason Shenai

We didn't cry; we opened the tin of biscuits. It was a large, square tin, Huntley & Palmer I seem to remember. The first biscuit I picked out had 'Victoria' written on it.

Had they buried her? Had they put her in an incinerator? The doctors wouldn't answer. Think of it as a miscarriage, they said. How could I? She had been mine; she had lived inside me and out. I would rather have gone to prison for not paying my tax than to have lost her.

Where is she now?

*   *   *

Victoria was gone and Pierre was soon to go. He was in love with someone else and my time was up. We parted – there is never any point in fighting a force as powerful as love.

15

MY MARRIAGE was over, Victoria was dead, but I still had
Christopher, well and strong, and back in London my
gynaecologist gave me some sound advice.

'Best to work. Keep busy. Keep working.'

The B.B.C. were to start serializing Anthony Trollope's
Palliser novels. The part of Lady Glencora Palliser had
already been cast twice but for some reason, at the eleventh
hour, both leading ladies had withdrawn and I was called
to the B.B.C. with several other actresses to read for it.

I had rather hoped that, as there was a rush to find a
leading lady, and because I had by now done several classic
serials for the B.B.C. (*The First Churchills, Vanity Fair, What
Katy Did* and *The Forsyte Saga*), I would not have to go
through the awful business of reading. Before I got to the
interview, knowing I was bottom of the list anyway, I
pleaded not to read. But the B.B.C. was adamant. I must
read. Their attitude puzzled me but I managed to be
philosophical about it, and I took twelve scripts away to
study – all that were ready. A few days later I was re-
prieved. The B.B.C. rang to say that they would like me to
play the part. Neither the producer, nor any of the directors
really wanted me, but *Time Life*, who were putting up a
percentage of the money, did. So I had two weeks to helter
skelter through the six *Palliser* novels – each novel containing roughly 300,000 words – literally squeeze into the

clothes and wigs made for the previous leading lady, and make some instant decisions about the part of Glencora which spanned thirty years of her life over twenty-six episodes.

Reading the six *Palliser* novels – all very long – would have been hard for me given unlimited time; to get through them in two weeks was impossible. The only way seemed to be to read all night, skipping every other chapter, and hoping to fall on the parts that referred to Glencora and Plantaganet Palliser, the two characters who provided the main thread in the narrative. The narrative spread over six novels and it would have taken even a fast reader quite a long time to get through them all. I have always been proud of the fact that I managed to read about one and a half million words of the *Palliser* books in just two weeks. For me, it was quite a feat.

When playing a character in a television series over many months, I often grow to feel very passionately about her. In the 'Saga' I was constantly suggesting that Fleur Forsyte should do this or that scene from the book to help enrich her character. I did the same in *The Pallisers*, but with more difficulty, as I did not find Trollope such easy reading as Galsworthy, nor was the character of Glencora as deeply written as that of Fleur. But Simon Raven, who did the adaptation, was a delight to work with and we developed scenes to flesh out the characters of Glencora and Plantaganet.

I also carried out my own research into the period and background, as I always do in television series, especially historical series. In fact, though I say it myself, the research I have done over the years has been phenomenal, given that reading alone is a torture. I suppose the most research I ever did was for *The First Churchills*, wading through both volumes of Sir Winston Churchill's biography of the First Duke of Marlborough, plus every available book on Queen Anne. I do not limit my research to visiting museums and historic houses, often I talk to the descendants of historical characters I am playing.

I remember that when I was researching for *The First Churchills*, I went up to Althorp to meet the late Earl Spencer, who as well as being Lady Diana Spencer's, now the Princess of Wales, grandfather, was a descendant of John and Sarah Churchill, the first Duke and Duchess of Marlborough. He kindly offered to show me the first Duchess's silver, including the solid silver canteen the great Duke had taken to war with him. I was fascinated by the superb articles that Sarah Churchill had commissioned in tortoiseshell and ivory for her dressing-table, which showed that she had been a woman of exquisite taste as well as of drive, determination, and loyalty. Earl Spencer gave me tea and I was just about to leave when he began talking about his son, the present Earl, and his grandchildren, including the Princess of Wales. 'They're such little things to be brought up without a mother,' he said with a sigh. 'But there we are.'

By the time *The Pallisers* was finished I was at a very low ebb. My life seemed to consist of nothing but continuous worries. I had not fully recovered from Victoria's death; there was the distress of my divorce from Pierre; there was my failure to come out into the open completely about my dyslexia. I felt utterly lost. The only solid things in my life were my son and my work, and even here I was plagued by doubt and lack of confidence.

Actors who have not been to drama school often experience feelings of inferiority and self-questioning – What have I missed? What would I have learnt? I was no exception.

One result of this deep unease about my abilities was that I kept working to improve the range of my voice. Everyday I practised the exercises that Iris Warren had given me in the sixties. Iris had helped me to read poetry and to sight-read songs as she played the rhythm with one finger on the piano. And she had taught me much else. 'Always watch things grow,' she would say, 'never lose contact with earth.' She had planted a seed in me that had grown into a passion for gardening, including growing my own vegetables. But Iris had died years earlier, and friends suggested that I should try a new teacher, Mr Saxstone (now dead), a man of Scots origin who had just moved back to England after many years teaching in New York. Mr Saxstone was apparently himself a dyslexic and claimed to have devised a method of helping dyslexics through music. I was ready to try anything, so I rang him to make an appointment for a lesson. His reply should have warned me.

'I would rather meet you for lunch,' he said, 'and then we can decide about the lessons,' and mentioned a quiet hotel round the corner from my London home. It seemed a little unusual, but I agreed.

As I drove up to the hotel I saw a tubby man waiting on the steps dressed in an open-necked denim shirt, a black suit, and odd shoes.

I parked the car and, as I walked over to the hotel, the man in the dark suit rushed down the steps to greet me. As he said 'hello', he fell down the last two steps and knocked me over. I landed on the bonnet of a stationary car.

Mr Saxstone picked himself up and introduced himself; then we hobbled into the restaurant. As we entered Mr Saxstone slipped again, fell, and sent the sweet trolley gliding to the other end of the room, where it cannoned into the buffet. No-one stopped its unimpaired flight, as everyone, including myself, was picking up, brushing down and checking the limbs of Mr Saxstone. In some confusion we finally managed to get safely to our table.

'Now, what will you eat my dear?' he said. 'You should eat. You look very thin and that is why you are having trouble with your voice and brain.'

'I'm not exactly having *trouble* with my voice. I just wish to improve it.'

'You're too thin,' he persisted. 'That's the cause of the trouble.'

I didn't argue, and we proceeded with the first course. Mr Saxstone knocked my water into my hors d'oeuvres with his sleeve as he 'politely' grabbed the salt to pass it to me. He then started shaking the salt on to my food, saying, 'You must have salt. Makes things nice and tasty. In America food has no taste – so I always used plenty of salt'.

'Your play,' he said abruptly. 'I should like to see it.'

'No, don't trouble yourself, the seats are very expensive.'

'I can afford it. Anyway, then I can tell you what I can do for you.'

'I'm not so sure lessons are really the right thing,' I said hesitantly. 'For me, I mean.' Pause. 'With a man,' I added.

'Don't be nervous, dear.' He clutched my arm.

'It's not that I'm nervous, but I respond better to women teachers. Probably something to do with my mother.'

He looked at me with new interest. 'Are you timid with men?'

I ploughed on. 'You see Cecily Berry is one of the best teachers in England. She's with the R.S.C. And although I know she's too busy to help me at the moment, I feel that perhaps I should wait.'

He clasped his hands round my forearm so strongly that I dropped my glass of wine.

'That *was* careless of you. Are you nervous?'

'No,' I said, 'are you?'

'You see I am a man of sixty. And I have never been married.' (Here we go, I thought.) 'I have lived a celibate life. There have been opportunities, of course. Many of my pupils have eyed me. But I have always resisted. Some of them have been deeply in love with me, though they've never told me so.'

'Then how do you know?'

'You can tell with women. But I have always resisted. I always knew that when I met the right girl, I would get married. You seem a lonely sort, and kind. Would you consider me? You are a nice girl, not like so many of the students I teach. Tarts – all of them. Tarts. Loose women. But you are a dyslexic, and I can tell that you are a nice girl.'

I gazed at him.

'I earn good money,' he said.

'But I came to talk to you about my voice.'

He didn't listen. 'Good money,' he repeated. 'Tax-free sometimes. I can keep you and your son. You don't seem to be doing very well . . .' [I was enjoying one of the best patches in my working life.] '. . . I could give you and your son stability. And meanwhile I can help you solve your problems. Working my way, with music, will give you confidence. Even your dyslexia will go.'

This was the third such proposition I had had in the last twelve months – all from weirdos. I was at a loss for words.

'Think about it,' Mr Saxstone said. 'Give yourself time. I know how a girl feels at a moment like this. I'll wait. I'll always wait.'

'Er – do you think we could get the bill? I must rush. I've got to collect Christopher from school.'

'We could do that together if we were married.'

'Let's get the bill. Please.'

He ignored this. 'I live with my mother, my sister and my brother, who is very religious – I approve of that. I am very religious myself. Now, here's a shock,' he leaned forward, 'My sister, she's a bit of a one, she's *very* naughty. Do you get me? Need I say more?'

'No. Of course not. Now I really must go.'

Mr Saxstone rose abruptly and knocked the entire table over – china and cutlery everywhere. The whole restaurant gazed at us in stunned silence.

I almost ran out and headed for my car, with Mr Saxstone chasing after me shouting, 'I'll see your play, then I'll tell you what I think.'

I snapped the door of my car shut.

'Wait, wait,' he said. 'I'll see your play,' and he banged his fist so hard on the bonnet of the car that he made a large dent in the metal.

I couldn't believe it. I reversed, shot off, drove straight home and wrote an impassioned letter to Cecily Berry pleading for lessons.

She agreed, and later Dennis Dowling and Catherine

Lambert gave me singing lessons. So the bizarre Mr Sax-stone had served one useful purpose at least.

❧ 16 ❧

MY BRUSH with Mr Saxstone was one of many similar shocks I had to cope with in the first years after my divorce. I suppose people must have sensed how vulnerable I was.

My conscience told me that I should publicly declare myself to be dyslexic so that I could help in the crusade to aid other dyslexics. But still I could not find the courage to do so.

Only among the medical profession was the word out; I had been asked to go to America to speak to the twenty-fifth meeting of the Orton Society in Minnesota, and describe my own personal experience of dyslexia. But I had been too frightened to go.

I felt deeply that I should start admitting I was dyslexic in the newspapers, on television, at work, to friends, but it was a daunting risk, professionally. Most people knew little about dyslexia, and since most people tend to be frightened of the unknown, the label 'dyslexic' could easily have meant permanent unemployment for me. My agent was, at first, very much against my admitting it.

'I can hear them saying it,' she said, ' "Susan Hampshire? Good god, no. She's dyslexic. Can't talk properly. She's bound to forget her lines or fall off the stage or something. We can't use her." '

Yet the feeling I had grew and grew that people with dyslexia, especially people in the public eye, should admit it, so that ultimately, when it was seen and known what a large percentage of people were sufferers, something positive could be done for them.

In 1975 an opportunity to do just this came my way. Frank Dale of the B.B.C. asked me to take part in a documentary about dyslexia for *Horizon*, called *If You Knew Suzie*. The Suzie in the story was not me, but Susan Alcock, a bright young dyslexic; I was merely to front the programme. This documentary put me in touch for the first time with the Dyslexia Institute.

The Institute had originated with a handful of professional people who, in the first half of this century, had become aware of the existence of a specific learning problem in otherwise normal children. During the 1960s, parent-groups were formed, demanding that the problems of dyslexia in their children should be identified and given specialist help. A new awareness soon revealed that specialist teachers were very scarce; ordinary remedial help, however good, was totally inappropriate to the dyslexic's needs. In 1963 the Invalid Children's Aid Association, with the help of a research grant, opened the Word Blind Centre. As the only centre in Britain where authoritative help and information was available, its fame spread. When it closed in 1970, through lack of funds, the North Surrey Dyslexic Society, seeing a desperate need for alternative help, set up a planning committee under the chairmanship of Mrs Sandhya Naidoo. After two years, a small teaching unit opened under the direction of Miss Kathleen Hickey, an inspired and gifted teacher, who had studied American methods.

It was a revelation to me when I discovered that this method of teaching and the little code I used on my scripts had great similarities. They too used pictures to illustrate a word and break it up into syllables.

Fronting *If You Knew Suzie*, I felt for the first time that I was actually doing something to help other dyslexics. I was thrilled to have the right opportunity openly to admit I was dyslexic, while being part of a programme that was constructive and helpful to other dyslexics – which it proved to be by the thousands of letters received afterwards.

Being the presenter on a documentary is not simply a matter of interviewing people; it also involves making fairly lengthy speeches to camera, filling the audience in on where you are, who you are just about to meet, their background, and so on. Usually this is done with the aid of a teleprompter – and here my old problem cropped up again. I had to learn all my speeches by heart, and since they kept making last-minute changes to the script it was gruelling work.

During the filming, in November 1975, we went to the University College of North Wales to interview Professor T. R. Miles. This was my second meeting with Tim Miles, the first having been at the Kershaw Committee. I did some more tests (see Appendix 1) and he gave a final confirmation that I was dyslexic.

I felt that, at last, a major breakthrough had occurred, thanks to the B.B.C. I was happy that the 'cat was out of the bag' and that I was publicly committed. My involvement with the Dyslexia Institute grew, although I did not at this point start remedial treatment for myself; but I was hopeful that one day I would, so that in my old age I could read and write with ease.

All my fears that publicly admitting I was dyslexic would be professional suicide proved to have been unfounded. My agent's telephone didn't stop ringing; and I was even asked to read in public!

On one occasion I was called in at the last minute to read some poems by Sir John Betjeman in Westminster Cathedral before Prince Philip. He was amazed to hear, afterwards, that I'd learnt the poems, not read them, and I explained to him about dyslexia. On another occasion, in Westminster Abbey, Flora Robson, Richard Baker and I had to read the lessons. I felt it would look wrong if it appeared that I'd learnt it, so I rehearsed with the Bible open in front of me in the pulpit. But the print was far too small for me to read easily and I became confused between what I'd learnt and what I was trying to read. Taking a tip from a high-up member of the Church, I covered the Bible with a piece of blank paper and then, on arrival in the pulpit, pretended to read the lesson. This was taking a huge risk as, nerves being what they are, should my mind have gone dead there would have been no way of prompting myself. Next time, I must have a blank paper with a few 'clues' written on it.

Reading numbers is no less difficult for me than reading words. I was once asked to present the cheque to a pools winner. There was a large reception in a great hotel, with the Press out in force. I got up to the microphone and said innocently, 'Mr James is the lucky winner who has just won a cheque for six hundred and ninety six pounds.'

I waited for the thunder of applause. Nothing. There was an audible groan from Mr James, and shufflings among the Press. An agitated official came to me and looked at the cheque.

'I'm so sorry,' I announced. 'You see I'm dyslexic, the other day I bought a nightie for thirty pounds. I thought it was a terrific bargain until I got my bank statement and found it had cost three hundred! However, we are not here to discuss my dyslexia or my nightie, we are here to present six thousand and ninety-six pounds to Mr James.'

Another groan from Mr James, and the official tried to wrench the cheque and the microphone from me. I clung to the microphone, looking very silly, feeling hot, and, blushing all over, I dropped the cheque. When I picked it up it was upside down – not that it made much difference to me.

'I'm so sorry,' I said, 'I've got it wrong again. It's six, zero, zero, comma, six, nine, zero.'

Someone took the microphone from me and announced, 'It's six hundred thousand, six hundred and ninety pounds for Mr James.'

At last applause burst out – and much relieved laughter. But when I handed Mr James his cheque I saw him checking and re-checking it.

Most English directors have heard through the grape-vine, or my agent, that I'm the actress who doesn't like to read and it is a form of notoriety that I often find embarrassing. But among certain directors I have discovered extraordinary sympathy and understanding. When I was asked to do a play directed by Simone Benmussa from the Jean Louis Barrault Company in Paris, I realized that she probably didn't know that I would find reading the play aloud difficult. Yet I felt that I had to warn her before the first day – but warn her without putting her off. I thought and thought. Maybe I wouldn't warn her at all and she'd just think I was nervous or had forgotten my glasses. But no – those sorts of subterfuges belonged to the past. I summoned up all my courage and telephoned her direct in Paris.

'Simone, I have something to tell you . . .'

'You don't like the play?'

'No, it's not that. It's just that . . . I don't know if you've heard . . . but I'm not a very good reader. I mean, on the first reading you may be so embarrassed you may want to sack me. I beg you, don't! It will be awful for you to listen to me as the part's so long – but I'll learn it within three days and then you'll see.'

'Suzanne,' she said, 'I knew you did not read very well. There was an article in *France Soir* about it.'

Everyone knows, I thought. And then she said, 'Anyway – I think I'm a little dyslexic myself!'

Just before we went into rehearsal the producer, Richard Jackson, invited me to supper to talk about the play.

'I can't,' I said, 'I must work and prepare for the first reading.'

'But you've had the script a week.'

'I know but you must realize after knowing me all these years that I must work and work for days and nights before a first reading.'

'Oh surely, Susan,' he said, 'you won't be nervous, not with all your experience.'

He still didn't understand.

'It's not a question of being nervous, I can't bear people to hear me read badly.'

The point is that even if someone has known me for seventeen years, they still cannot appreciate that reading aloud is difficult, and a great strain on me.

Each director has a different approach. Clifford Williams, at the first reading of Shaw's *Man and Superman* for the R.S.C. which Eddie Kulukundis (now my husband) presented at the Savoy, leaned gently over me and said, 'I'd like to read through this first bit – if you can see the words.'

'I can see the words,' I explained, 'but usually in the wrong order. But don't worry, Clifford, I've learned it, so let's read.'

When I was playing in *Tribades* by Per Olof Enquist at the Hampstead Theatre, Michael Rudman declared in his delicious transatlantic accent, 'Well we all know Susan can't read – she tells us often enough, of course, we don't believe her – she'll do anything for attention – so let's read the play non-stop for the next two days!' We did. Actors will take almost anything from a good director.

I remember taking part in an A.T.V. programme, based on some of the letters in Antonia Fraser's book *Love Letters*, with Richard Johnson and Cleo Laine. At the first reading Richard Johnson read with ease, Cleo with glasses, and I with a red face, as several of my pages had got stuck together and I hadn't pre-learned the part.

Antonia, knowing my problem, said she'd read the letters for me. Later, when we were discussing a particularly heartbreaking letter from Rosamond Lehmann's book, *Dusty Answer,* she asked if I knew the background to the letter.

'No, I'm afraid I don't – I've not read it,' I said.

Immediately Antonia opened the book and read perfectly and effortlessly, allowing me to glean the information without embarrassment. Some people make everything easy. There was no fuss – she just picked up the book and read the passage to me – beautifully.

It was only towards the end of writing this book, when I was thinking about all those readings, and the problems they had caused me over the years, that a dim memory came to me – a memory of reading for the part of Raina in Shaw's *Arms And The Man*. I could vividly remember the scene in my agent's office after the audition, but the audition itself was pretty well a blank, no doubt because I had deliberately erased it from my mind. All I knew was that it had something to do with Joss Ackland.

Joss Ackland happens to be a close friend of my new husband, Eddie, and when he heard that we were going to get married he told him about a terrible audition that I once gave back in the early Sixties. I record it here not only to show by contrast how much I've improved since, but as a reminder of the problems other dyslexics face every day.

Joss was to direct the play at the Mermaid Theatre, and, because of some change in the schedule, it had to be cast in two and a half days. I was sent along to audition by my agent and, naturally, at that stage of my career, I was over-awed by the thought of reading for a *Shaw* play, and was not particularly keen to go. (This account is made up partly of my own indistinct recollections and partly of Joss's much more vivid ones!)

When I got to the audition Joss asked me to read Raina while he read Bluntschli, the part he was to play. This was perfectly normal procedure.

I started to pace up and down the room, script in hand, looking desperately out of the window.

'Fine, fine,' I said, 'I'll read. Just give me time.' And I continued to pace up and down, not reading a word. This went on for ages. I had the book open in front of me and I was staring at the page, breathing deeply, but unable to utter.

'There's plenty of time,' Joss said patiently. 'Just relax. Take your time. There's no hurry.' (There was, of course.)

Suddenly I blurted out, 'I can't. I just can't do it. I can't.'

Joss told me not to worry, to go away, have lunch, look at the script, and come back at two-thirty.

When I returned, Joss said, 'Now. Relax. Go to the window, pick up the script, and read it as though you were reading a newspaper.'

There was a long pause. I held the script in my hand and looked out of the window at the Thames, and the boats moored along the quays. Then I said, 'I can't. I just can't do it.'

Obviously I had made no attempt to learn the speeches over lunch, so daunted had I been by the thought of reading Shaw. I had already admitted defeat.

After ten minutes of patient cajoling by Joss and, no doubt, tearful protests from me, the audition was abandoned – but only until the next day.

'Go home,' Joss said, 'take the script with you, and come back tomorrow at half past nine and we'll have another go.'

On the following day I arrived at the Mermaid to be informed that Joss was in another building.

'Go over to fifty-two,' I was told. When I arrived Joss was in a meeting. They told him I was there and he came rushing out of his office and down the stairs at full speed. He slipped, fell, and sprained his ankle.

In great pain he hobbled back to the theatre with me, and with one trouser leg rolled up to his knee, and his bad foot in a bucket of water, we began the reading. At least he did. I just sat in silence, shaking my head, and saying, 'I can't. I just can't.'

In the end he let me go.

What I cannot understand is why I had not learned the part overnight. What was so terrifying about this particular play? Or was it just that I secretly feared that I was not capable of doing the part justice?

The rest of the story I remember only too painfully. I went to my agent's office and saw Robin Fox, Ros Chatto's boss. I told him that I didn't want the part of Raina, not mentioning, of course, that I had not been able to read for it. Robin stared at me. This was one of the first opportunities that I had had of playing a classic role and I was throwing it away.

'Who the hell do you think you are?' he said at last. 'God?'

I didn't reply. I rose from the sofa – I can still remember how soft it was – and left the room. The lump in my throat hurt me. I felt that his attitude was terribly unfair; and so it would have been had I had the courage to tell him my secret.

I walked down Regent Street, past Verrey's, blinded with tears, that phrase – 'Who do you think you are – God?' – ringing in my ears.

It had been a disaster for me, and not so good for Joss either, who had to play Bluntschli with a bandaged ankle and using a stick. He was in great pain throughout every performance. He still gets pain to this day, and declares, 'I still think of you, Susan, and dyslexia when my ankle gives me trouble.'

About ten years later I did play Raina in *Arms And The Man*, but in Hong Kong during the Festival. Eddie Kulukundis saw the production and wanted to bring it to the West End. I remember saying to him:

'I don't want to play Raina in London. I'm too old for the part. I should have done it ten years ago.'

I had absolutely no recollection at all of having failed to do just that a decade earlier.

17

APPEARING IN *If You Knew Suzie* brought about a major change in my life; I became closely involved with the dyslexia cause. I raise as much money as I can for existing Dyslexia Institutes and to finance new ones, and add my voice to those who are trying to persuade the Government to organize compulsory screening for all children entering primary school. If only there was automatic screening, at three or five, the estimated twelve per cent of the population who suffer from dyslexia would not have to suffer unnecessarily, because they do not fit into the educational system as it stands. After all, why should an hereditary disability not be accommodated, especially as one in eight is such a large proportion of the population?

Since the showing of that first documentary, and others on the same lines, the attitude to the problem is improving, judging by the hundreds of letters I have received from fellow dyslexics. Yet the sorry fact remains that provision for dyslexics in state schools is still nil. In some public schools allowances are made for dyslexics in exams, and remedial help is available. The headmaster of the City of London School, for instance, is thoroughly aware of dyslexia. According to him, three per cent of his boys are dyslexic. Because their problem is identified and understood, most of them leave the school with flying colours, and go on to University and distinguished careers.

Part of the problem is, of course, that so many people, including teachers and doctors, simply refuse to admit that dyslexia even exists. It is branded as 'the middle-class disease', dismissed as an 'excuse' dreamed up by parents who cannot face the truth that their children are merely dunces. Another convenient way of shrugging off dyslexia is to say, 'Oh, it's obviously a psychological problem. Children who can't read and write properly are obviously disturbed in some way. They need psychologists not special teachers.'

None of this is true. Scientists are now almost certain that dyslexia is caused by abnormalities in cell structure of the brain in the areas that control language. I quote from an article published in November 1979 in the *Boston Globe*:

Researchers have found the first physical evidence that some forms of the learning disorder known as dyslexia may result from specific abnormalities in the brain, according to results released by the Beth Israel Hospital in Boston.

Dr Anthony Galaburda and Dr Thomas Kemper, neurologists at Beth Israel, made the discoveries in the brain of a twenty-year-old man killed in an accident. The victim, who grew up in a Boston suburb, graduated from high school with the reading level of a fourth-grader.

'Dyslexia has been thought to be a psychological problem but it is really a neurological abnormality,' Galaburda said. 'Our study shows for the first time that there are actual differences in the anatomy of the brain of a dyslexic person.'

Their work found 'striking' abnormalities in the layers of the cells in the left cerebral hemisphere, considered responsible for language functions.

'This finding is very major,' said Dr Norman Geschwind, head of Beth Israel's neurological laboratory. 'Obviously this is only one case, but the changes found in the brain in this particular case are nothing borderline.

They are striking and clear cut. The abnormalities cannot be the result of postbirth difficulties. The boy was born with them, with the way the brain was put together.

'In addition, areas that were abnormal were found only on the left side, the language side, and the abnormal areas were found in the language sectors.'

In the face of such evidence, one might expect the sceptics to be confounded. But there is yet another prejudice that dyslexics, and those who try to help them, have to combat. This is the deep-rooted idea that all learning, all education, any expression of ideas, must be done through language, through words. The idea that it is possible to learn and communicate *visually*, through colour and shape, seems to be a heresy, though it is one that naturally occurs to dyslexics. It is, after all, the basis of the code I developed to cope with the problems of reading scripts. Much of the potential in dyslexic children is stamped out by the rigid appliance of the rules of literacy, simply because they work for the majority. Yet some very impressive intelligences have seen the value of visual learning and communication.

Leonardo da Vinci wrote, in referring to his detailed anatomical drawings which he made for his own research, 'No one could hope to convey so much true knowledge without an immense, tedious and confused length of writing and time, except through this very short way of drawing from different aspects.'

Bertrand Russell wrote in his *Analysis of Mind*, 'Those who have a relatively direct vision of facts are often incapable of translating their vision into words, while those who possess the words have usually lost the vision. It is partly for this reason that the highest philosophical capacity is so rare; it requires a combination of vision with abstract words, which is hard to achieve and too quickly lost in the few who have, for a moment, achieved it.'

This would indicate that the way lies open for learning not only through words. An article in the *New Era Journal of World Fellowship of Education*, published in February 1981, states: 'It is now just as easy to transmit a direct vision of facts as it is to convey information about the same subject through words. Photography, film, television and high speed offset lithography and photogravure are readily available and the costs involved for the production of the visual image compare very favourably with the purely verbal one.'

'Why be literate?' asked a headline in *The Observer* of 7 February 1973:

Most illiterates only want to learn to read because it is the accepted thing to do – because the rest of us make them feel ashamed. We've all been socialised into thinking that reading is not only necessary but positively virtuous. But in fact it is holding us back. Radio and television have turned newspapers and news-periodicals into anachronisms. And now modern cassette-players and audio-visual aids are doing the same to the whole concept of the written word. So why go on burdening people with unnecessary skills? If only people would open their eyes and stop living in the past, life could be so much easier and more pleasurable.

This, I think, rather overstates the case. Most dyslexics long to be able to read – I certainly did – and the point is that fresh approaches, through visual aids, can help them to do it.

Until I became actively involved, I had no idea what a battle it is to persuade the authorities not only that dyslexia exists, and is widespread, but to get backing for new ideas in combating it. But a battle it is.

Professor Miles campaigns in the North, Margaret Newton of Birmingham University in the Midlands, Helen Arkell, McDonald Critchley and Mrs Beve Hornsby in the South, and Marion Welchman in the West, while the Dyslexia Institute covers overall strategy. Beyond this, there are little pockets of people throughout England, not under any umbrella, battling on their own – an individual mother working quietly at home with her child, an isolated teacher in a village school believing and helping. But all is far from bright. In early 1980 a teacher from the North bounced into my dressing-room at the Phoenix Theatre, after a performance of *Night and Day*. 'This dyslexic thing you say you are. I'm a sceptic. Don't believe in it. I teach children and I know the bright ones from the lazy or emotionally disturbed ones. Dyslexia is just laziness or bad teaching. Look at you, you wouldn't be able to do this Tom Stoppard stuff if you were really dyslexic.'

I wanted to seize her by the throat and scream at her, 'Read *The Dyslexic Child* by Professor Miles and *Reversals* by Eileen Simpson and then tell me you're a sceptic, then tell me a dyslexic is mentally retarded or lazy or badly taught. See if you don't realize, for the first time in your life, that you, like many of the educated public, are confused in your own mind when you assume that spelling and reading are inexorably linked to a person's intelligence.'

I wanted to tell her that it had only been my own dogged refusal to admit that I had a disability that had forced me to read and spell with a degree of respectability. I wanted to tell her about the dyslexic's deep-rooted sense of inferiority, the longing to be thought unintelligent no longer, the desire to tap the knowledge in his mind at will, the frustration of battling with the evaporating thought.

I have many faults but self-pity is not one of them. Frustration, yes. Boiling blood at the helplessness of so many, yes. But anger gets one nowhere; action is what counts, which is why I do my best to support the Dyslexia Institute, remedial teaching, coloured books, oral exams and anything that can compensate for what the dyslexic misses; confidence, books, knowledge, dignity.

When I read Professor Miles's *The Dyslexic Child*, written with such compassion and depth (it should be compulsory reading for teachers and parents), I thought to myself,

'Have I been going through all that?'

It was obviously too late to repair the damage done to my intellect, but not too late to make sure that others, with a less cushioned background, should not suffer. When Society allows a dyslexic to sink, through ignorance or prejudice, it is not only the dyslexic who loses. Society loses as well. There are so many examples of young people who, in the last two or three decades, have licked the problem, overcome it, or managed, with superb determination, to live with it. There's nothing like an obstacle to enrich life! My own life has encompassed more than I ever expected in my wildest dreams, and my small achievements have been far beyond anything I ever expected.

Richard Rogers, for instance, is the architect who has designed, among other things, the much hailed Pompidou Centre in Paris. At sixteen he was told, 'The most you can expect is to be a policeman in South Africa.' Duncan Goodhew, the Olympic Silver Medal swimmer, is another inspiration. Because he was always called Duncan the Dunce at school, he was determined to shine in another field. He did. Nikita Lonabo, Senior Vice President of the International Resources & Finance Bank, is a brilliant banker who employs a secretary to correct his spelling – but he boldly leaves mis-spelt messages for his high-powered colleagues. Having established his brilliance in his field, he has nothing to fear.

The list of 'survivors' is long, but that of the millions throughout the world who, because of the rough beginning and permanently damaged confidence, fall by the wayside is infinitely longer.

Last spring I was at the opening of the new Dyslexia Institute in Lincoln and, chatting with the children, some of whom had already started remedial schooling, others of whom were to begin classes the following week, I was struck by the difference between them. I looked at the little confident faces of the ones getting help – seeing the light for the first time and feeling they were not beyond hope.

Then I looked at the tight withdrawn expressions of the others. Their personalities lacked all confidence; they were children who could not believe that they would ever be like other children, or ever escape from the quicksand swallowing them.

How vividly these tragic faces brought back my own childhood, and how wonderful it was to feel that now, at last, there was hope for them, and that they could have what my mother gave me – patience, understanding and care.

*   *   *

Over the years many people (apart from Mr Saxstone!) have written to me saying that they could teach me to read with ease. But the plans they laid out on paper never really got any response from my gut. Watching the teachers work at the Dyslexia Institute, and sitting through several classes, I realized that if I could take the time to go back to zero, and go to classes twice a week for a year or so, I could re-learn to spell correctly and re-learn to read.

To read with ease, instead of fighting to read, would be wonderful. I should go back and start from scratch, for the world of books is not quite closed to me and I would so love to read without trying.

In 1980 *The Sunday Times* asked me to review Eileen Simpson's book, *Reversals*, an American woman's autobiographical account of dyslexia. When I'd finished the book I came away with one very strong conclusion and one very acute question. The conclusion was: don't ask the halt to review a book about the lame. Eileen Simpson's 'lameness' was so familiar to me that it held no mystery and I tended to underestimate her achievement in overcoming it. The question, prompted by the fact that Eileen Simpson had discovered and enjoyed a very difficult writer like James Joyce, was, 'Why can't I?'

I felt that I could not let another day pass with the world

of books more or less closed to me. I had made a certain amount of progress through the years, but it is not good enough. After all I have an extremely intelligent young son, who is constantly demanding answers. 'I don't know. Look it up in the Encyclopaedia' is a way out that satisfies me less and less.

18

HAVING WRITTEN at some length about the obstacles dyslexia puts in the way of earning a living, I realize that I have said very little about the ordinary, day-to-day problems of being a dyslexic.

Some of these I regard as quite serious. For instance, the sad truth is that I have hardly ever read my son a bedtime story. When he was very tiny, I used to make up stories as I went along, rather than read them. This method didn't last long. I found the creative effort tiring and Christopher found the stories annoying, as they usually had a moral to them, like the one about the little boy who wouldn't tidy up his toys and wasn't allowed to go to the moon with his friends. I tried to read to him, but he found the experience exasperating. I remember picking my way through a Christopher Robin story. Christopher kept correcting me, 'No, Mummy, that's not right, that's not what happens there. Have you missed a bit?'

I gave up in the end and so Christopher has missed out on that all-important ten minutes of ritual and intimacy before sleep.

Dyslexia even affects my cooking. I enjoy cooking, and am a moderately good cook, but people are forever complaining that I stick to the same old dishes, again and again. It is true, alas, and the reason is simple: I cannot use recipes! Whenever I have tried I have completely misread them and dishes have burned to a crisp in the oven because I put them in for 'three to four hours' instead of for three-quarters of an hour.

The only way I can learn a new recipe is to persuade a friend to stand in the kitchen and tell me exactly what to do, what ingredients to put in, and how to cook them. Once I have a recipe in my mind it is there forever, and if I do forget some detail I ring up and ask. I *never* look it up in a recipe book. Often, too, I just invent new recipes, and that I enjoy most of all.

As well as these major problems, there are a mass of minor irritations in every day – in every hour, in fact – that are directly attributable to dyslexia. To illustrate these, here is a diary of a typical day. It could be called 'A Day In The Life of a Dyslexic'.

*　　*　　*

7.30 Christopher comes into the bedroom wanting me to check his homework. As it's English homework, and Eddie, who usually helps, is on a long-distance call, I have to ring up my sister Jane (who runs the school) on the other line
8.00 The post arrives. Half the letters are from charities, and are over two pages long. I cannot possibly cope with them at breakfast time, so I have to put them aside to study later when I can find a moment of absolute peace and quiet.
10.00 Shopping. I can't check my change fast enough. Only when I've left the shop do I realize that I've paid 35p too much.
11.00 To the Post Office to collect my Child Allowance. I have to fill in a form so that the book can be registered in my new married name. I can't do it on the spot because the form is long and complicated. I have to take it home so that Eddie can check it tonight.
12.00 I have promised to give a buffet lunch for a charity meeting at home, to raise money for Population Concern. I have forgotten to prepare the mayonnaise, so I have to

ring my sister Ann to remind me how to do it. Normally Christopher holds the phone and relays the information to me in the kitchen, but he's at school. I rush from the phone to the kitchen, from the kitchen to the phone. It is *not* the best way to make mayonnaise.

3.00 Eddie rings to ask me to get yesterday's *Financial Times* and read him the Stock Report. It takes me at least three tries to get it right.

4.00 Christopher's friends come to tea after school. One of the boys brings some medicine he's supposed to take. Panic! Have we read the instructions on the label correctly? I ring his home to check. His mother asks me if I could drive her son home as she has to wait for the plumber to arrive.

6.00 I look up the boy's street in the A-Z. We get into the car and I start navigating. I'm soon hopelessly lost. I phone his mother from a call box.

7.00 We arrive at last. It was a journey of only three miles!

7.15 I leave for the theatre and work in a terrible rush as a result of the delays.

7.30 A huge pile of letters awaits me at the Stage Door. I have to look through them in case any one of them is urgent. The letters from the morning's post are still in my bag, unread. I ask my dresser, Robin, to 'glance over them to see if there's anything urgent'. He kindly agrees – and I've saved myself three quarters of an hour of agony.

12.00 I get home to find that I've set the TV video recording machine all wrong and a documentary I particularly wanted to tape hasn't been recorded. Eddie comes in, with a letter. 'Oh, this came,' he says. I open it. It is from American Express. I had sent them a cheque which has been returned because the words and figures I wrote do not correspond! It's the third this week! The end of another day!

19

ABOUT A year ago there was a reunion of friends from my mother's school. We had all of us gone our separate, but equally interesting, ways and I was amazed to discover that none of the others remembered my having any special difficulty at school.

'Fancy your having problems at school. I don't remember that. You must have been brilliant at covering up. How on earth did you do it?'

'Oh,' I shrugged, 'I cheated a great deal and copied all of you, and when there was a real stumbling block I distracted the class with my hamster.'

They all remembered *that*!

'If I'd known,' I continued, 'that you hadn't noticed I was hopeless, perhaps I wouldn't have suffered so much! It's always the thought of "what will the others think?" that's so demoralizing. It may sound ridiculous but I thought if I had a certain number on my bus ticket, or if I didn't walk on the lines on the pavement outside the school, my work would be better. I thought good work was connected with good luck!'

'But you were always getting the Hard Work Cup and the Deportment Cup and the Handwriting Cup and the Art Cup.'

'I know. My family were amazingly good at contriving ways of encouraging me.'

'Yes, your mother *was* amazing, we all adored her. And she had such a positive influence on our lives. We were so lucky to have had such an imaginative headmistress. Come to that, you were even luckier to have had her as your mother. She was magic. Do you remember her funny Latin reading? Yet we all learned so much.'

'You do realize she was almost completely self-taught?' I asked. 'Yet she maintained as high a standard as any school in London.'

Simone Warner (née Nangle pronounced Tangle by my mother) chipped in, 'One thing I remember. You always used to spell your name as "S.H." '

'Well didn't you think that was odd?'

'I suppose I did. But there's something else I remember. The English teacher was always saying that you should write!'

*   *   *

My brother John would hardly have agreed with this view. When I told him I had nearly finished my book on dyslexia, he said with a chuckle, 'Good God, that's odd. Not only can't you write, but dyslexia's about the dullest subject in the world. Anyway, it's been done before.'

'Not by me.'

We laughed.

'Well, you'd better pep it up a bit.'

'I've no intention of "pepping it up",' I said, 'the subject is so little aired, the more written about it the better.'

'God help us.'

'It'll be interesting to other dyslexics, about eleven per cent of the population.'

'We'll see. Are they keeping in your spelling mistakes? I hope so!'

It had been the same when I told my sister Ann that I was starting a book.

After prolonged silence followed by laughter from the

other end of the telephone, I heard her ask: 'What about?'
I told her.

She laughed again, more nervously. I asked her: 'Can
you remember anything about teaching me when I was a
child? Anything that would be useful?'

'Well, I remember your singing well. You had a beautiful
voice. I taught you the Messiah.'

Pause. Then, 'How on earth are you going to do it?'

'How do you think? By just sitting down and writing it.'

After more laughter we got on to the safer subject of
our children and the merits of keeping goats in London.

My reception having been one of amazement, I decided
to drop the subject for a time and 'sat down and wrote'.
Then, some months later, I had tea with my other sister,
Jane, who is now the Principle of what used to be my
mother's school and with whom I'd had quite lucid discussions about dyslexia over the past few years. She had
been a sceptic.

'There's certainly not a pupil in this school that has it,' she
would say. But she had since had a change of attitude. When I
told her about the book, she said: 'Good, it needs to be done.'

I asked her what she could remember about teaching me.

'I remember that Ann and I were always buying you good
easy-to-read books when you were a child. I think they
helped. But what helped most of all was our encouraging
your acting.'

I told Christopher's father about the book while Christopher and I were holidaying at the Colombe d'Or in St
Paul de Vence and I was working on it.

'Wonderful!' he said. 'Simone Signoret wrote her book
in that hotel and she has made three hundred thousand
francs – maybe more!'

When I told Eddie, my new husband and probably the
kindest man in the world, that I had written a book, his
comment was, 'I'm going to arrange for you to take time
off and have a teacher from the Dyslexia Institute so you
can study for a year so then you might be able to read it!'

Assessing for Dyslexia*

IMPORTANT

It is very important that someone who later reads this form should have a record of exactly what happened. Use of a tick is in order if the subject gives the correct response instantaneously, but please record all delays and hesitations and always indicate if the subject asks for the question to be repeated, echoes the question, or tries to reorientate himself by repeating what went before. (Use the abbreviations RR = request for repetition, EQ = echoes the question, and EP = epanalepsis, taking up what he has already said.) Please do *not* put a cross if the answer is wrong, but record as accurately as possible *what the subject said*. Where appropriate, record any supplementary questions which you yourself ask.

Name.. Date................................

1 **Left-Right (body-parts)**

            Instruction   *S's response*

(a) Show me your right hand..
      (Did you have difficulty when you
          were younger?)..

(b) Show me your left ear..

(c) Touch your right ear with your left hand................(ear)................(hand)......

(d) (Putting hands on table)
      Which is *my* right hand?..

(e) Touch my left hand with your right hand..

(f) Point to my right ear with your left hand..

(g) Touch my right hand with your right hand..

(h) Point to my left eye with your right hand..

(i) Point to my left ear with your left hand..

(j) Touch my right hand with your left hand..

Special strategies:..

....

....

2 Repeating Polysyllabic Words

'I am going to say some words and I want you to say them after me'

S's Response

preliminary

philosophical

contemporaneous

anemone

statistical

3 Subtraction

			Response	*Time taken*
(a) What is:	9 take away 2		....	....
	6 ,, ,, 3		....	....
	19 ,, ,, 7		....	....
	24 ,, ,, 2		....	....
	52 ,, ,, 9		....	....
	44 ,, ,, 7		....	....

Record here whether the subject uses any 'concrete aids' (e.g. fingers or marks on paper) and/or any other interesting strategies:

....

....

....

4 Tables

Do they (did they) teach you tables at school? ....

Did you have any special difficulty in learning them? ....

Try your .... times table.

(Discontinue as soon as there is sufficient evidence for a 'plus'. In the absence of such evidence continue over *three* tables. These should normally be the 6, 7, and 8 times, but with younger children it is sometimes informative to ask for the 2, 3, and 4 times.)

continued

5 **Months of the year**

   (a) Say the months of the year ....

   ....

   (b) Now say them backwards ....

   ....

6 **Repeating Digits**
   'I am going to say some numbers, and when I have finished I want you to say them just as I said them.'

Series	Trial I	Trial II
(3)	3–8–6	6–1–2
(4)	3–4–1–7	6–1–5–8
(5)	8–4–2–3–9	5–2–1–8–6
(6)	3–8–9–1–7–4	7–9–6–4–8–3
(7)	5–1–7–4–2–3–8	9–8–5–2–1–6–3
(8)	1–6–4–5–9–7–6–3	2–9–7–6–3–1–5–4
(9)	5–3–8–7–1–2–4–6–9	4–2–6–9–1–7–8–3–5

   'I am going to say some more numbers, but this time when I have finished I want you to say them *backwards*. For example, if I say 9–2–7, what would you say?'

Series	Trial I	Trial II
(2)	2–5	6–3
(3)	5–7–4	2–5–9
(4)	7–2–9–6	8–4–9–3
(5)	4–1–3–5–7	9–7–8–5–2
(6)	1–6–5–2–9–8	3–6–7–1–9–4
(7)	8–5–9–2–3–4–2	4–5–7–9–2–8–1
(8)	6–9–1–6–3–2–5–8	3–1–7–9–5–4–8–2

7 **Evidence of dyslexia in other members of the family**

Summary

Name.. **Date of birth**..

Date of test.. Age on testing..

Reading Age .... (Test used ....)

Spelling Age .... (Test used ....)

Intelligence level
    (tick as appropriate)   Z Y X W V U

        Composite I.Q.
            or
        Selected I.Q.

	Highest pass	*Lowest failure*
Digits forward		
Digits reversed		

Evidence for dyslexia   + o —
    Digits forward
    Digits reversed
    Left-Right
    Polysyllables
    Subtraction
    Tables
    Months forward
    Months reversed
    b-d confusion
    Others in family affected

No. of 'pluses' out of 10   ....

Posner task   ....

Digit absorption

WISC	Similarities	Picture Completion
	Vocabulary	Block Design
	Comprehension	Object Assembly

---

* This test is reproduced from *The Clinical Picture of Dyslexia* by Professor T. Miles to be published in 1982 by Granada Publishing.

APPENDIX II

Sources of Information on Dyslexia

The Orton Dyslexia Society
724 York Road
Baltimore, MD 21204
(301) 296-0232

The Orton Dyslexia Society is a nonprofit scientific and educational organization for the study and treatment of individuals with dyslexia (specific language disability). The society, which was founded in 1949, is named for Dr. Samuel T. Orton, an American pioneer in the field. It has 25 branches, and members in all 50 states and around the world. Write to national headquarters (address above) for the branch nearest you.

The Orton Dyslexia Society publishes a variety of books, monographs, and other materials including the following.

The Bulletin of the Orton Society, a professional journal about Specific Language Disability. It is free to members; single copies and subscriptions are available, as are back issues.
"Perspectives on Dyslexia", the society's newsletter, is free to members.

Books

Reading, Writing and Speech Problems in Children by Samuel Torry Orton, M.D.
Reading, Perception and Language: Papers from the World Congress on Dyslexia, 1974, edited by Drake D. Duane, M.D., and Margaret Byrd Rawson
Sex Differences in Dyslexia edited by Alice Ansara, Norman Geschwind, Albert Galaburda, Marilyn Albert and Nanette Gartrell

Monographs

Dyslexia in Special Education compiled by Lucia Rooney Carnes, Ph.D.
Education and Specific Language Disability: The Papers of Anna Gillingham, M.A., 1919–1963, compiled by Sally B. Childs
The Dyslexic Child by Drake D. Duane, M.D., and Paula Dozier. A *Pediatric Annals* reprint

Information Packets

For Parents
For Educators
For Physicians

Reprints

A. Psychiatric Aspects of Language Disability by Leon Eisenberg, M.D. (from READING, PERCEPTION AND LANGUAGE)

B. Developmental Dyslexia: Educational Treatment and Results by Margaret Byrd Rawson. (from READING, PERCEPTION AND LANGUAGE)

2. "Can't Spell, Can't Read"
by J. Roswell Gallagher, M.D.

5. Specific Language Disability (Dyslexia)
by J. Roswell Gallagher, M.D.

6. Sound Reading
by Sally B. Childs

7. Diagnostic Considerations in Children with Reading Disability
By Archie A. Silver, M.D.

8. Practical Applications of Diagnostic Studies of Children with Specific Reading Disability
by Rosa A. Hagin, Ph.D.

9. Obscure Causes of School Failure—A Pediatric Viewpoint
by Raymond Clemmens, M.D.

11. The Orton-Gillingham Approach
by June Lyday Orton

12. Reading and Speech Problems as Expression of a Specific Language Disability
by Edwin M. Cole, M.D., and Louise Walker, B.A., LSC

13. Prognosis in Dyslexia
by Margaret B. Rawson

86.   Reading Disorders: Strategies for Recognition and Management
        by Leon Eisenberg, M.D.

88.   TWO SCHOOL PRINCIPALS SPEAK: Program Planning for
        Dyslexic Children in the General Classroom, by Genevieve
        G. Oliphant, Ph.D., and The School Principal as Advocate for
        the Child with Learning Differences by William Ellis

90.   Dyslexia: Evolution of a Concept
        by Arthur L. Benton, Ph.D.

91.   Learning to Read: an Unnatural Act
        by Philip B. Gough and Michael L. Hillinger

92.   Patterning and Organizational Deficits in Children with
        Language and Learning Disabilities
        by Katrina de Hirsch, F.C.S.T. and Jeannette J. Jansky, Ph.D.

93.   Written Language Disorders
        Regina Cicci, Ph.D.

94.   Persistent Auditory Disorders in Young Dyslexic Adults
        by Doris J. Johnson, Ph.D.

95.   A Diversity Model for Dyslexia
        by Margaret Byrd Rawson

96.   The Right Shift Theory of Handedness and Developmental
        Language Problems
        by Marian Annette

97.   Strategies for Initial Reading Instruction
        by Linda W. Camp, Nancy E. Winbury and Danielle Zinna

The following short bibliography is recommended by the New York Branch of the Orton Society, Inc.

Clark, Louise, *Can't Read, Can't Write, Can't Talk Too Good Either,* New York: Walker and Co., 1973.

Duane, Drake and Rome, Paula D., *The Dyslexic Child,* Educators Publishing Service, 75 Moulton St., Cambridge, Mass. 02138.

Osman, Betty B., *Learning Disabilities: A Family Affair,* New York: Random House, 1979.

Simpson, Eileen, *Reversals: A Personal Account of Victory Over Dyslexia,* Boston: Houghton-Mifflin, 1979.

Thompson, Lloyd J., *Reading Disability,* Springfield, Ill.: Charles C. Thomas, 1969.

Weiss, Helen Ginandes and Martin S., *Home Is A Learning Place,* Boston: Little, Brown, 1976.

Association for Children and Adults With Learning Disabilities
4156 Library Road
Pittsburgh, PA 15234
(412) 341-1515

This national, nonprofit organization was formed in 1964 by a group of concerned parents. It is the only national organization devoted to defining and finding solutions for the broad spectrum of learning problems. It has 50 state affiliates with more than 785 local chapters. Write to National Headquarters for the chapter nearest you. National Headquarters has a film rental service as well as a resource library of over 600 publications for sale, including the following dyslexia-related materials.

BENDER, L.	*50-Year Review of Dyslexia*
CLARK, L.	*Can't Read, Can't Write, Can't Talk Too Good Either*
DANENHOWER, H.	*Teaching Adults with Specific Language Disability*
DUANE/ROME	*Developmental Dyslexia*
EDGINGTON, R.	*Helping Children With Reading Disability*
FULLER/FRIEDRICH	*Three Diagnostic Patterns of Reading Disabilities*
GOLDBERG/SCHIFFMAN	*Dyslexia—Problems of Reading Disabilities*
GOLDSTEIN, H.	*Readings in Dyslexia*
GRIFFITHS, A.	*Teaching the Dyslexia Child*

LEVINSON, HAROLD, M.D.	*A Solution to the Riddle Dyslexia*
LISTON/CROSBY	*Dyslexia: What You Can & Can't Do About It*
SIMAK, C.	*Dyslexia: Disability is a Social Problem*
SIMULA, V.L.	*Anxiety and The Learning to Read Process*
SLINGERLAND, B.	*Meeting the Needs of Dyslexic Children*
SMITH, B.K.	*Dilemma of a Dyslexic Man*
WAGNER, R.	*Dyslexia and Your Child*
WILLIAMS, J.	*Dyslexia: The Modern Plague*
YOUNG, W.	*Enduring Mystery of Dyslexia (Readers Digest)*

"Newsbrief," the official ACLD newsletter, is published six times annually.

Information on dyslexia may also be obtained from:

Learning Disability Program
Bureau of Education for the Handicapped
U.S. Office of Education
Washington, D.C. 20202